Sunday Stories

A year of weekly devotionals
to encourage your walk with Jesus

By Janelle Weeks

All Scripture quotations, unless otherwise indicated, are taken from the Holy Bible, New International Version®, NIV®. Copyright ©1973, 1978, 1984, 2011 by Biblica, Inc.® Used by permission of Zondervan. All rights reserved worldwide. www.zondervan.com The "NIV" and "New International Version" are trademarks registered in the United States Patent and Trademark Office by Biblica, Inc.®

Scripture quotations taken from the (NASB®) New American Standard Bible®, Copyright © 1960, 1971, 1977, 1995, 2020 by The Lockman Foundation. Used by permission. All rights reserved. lockman.org

Scripture quotations marked (ESV) are taken from THE HOLY BIBLE, ENGLISH STANDARD VERSION®, Copyright© 2001 by Crossway, a publishing ministry of Good News Publishers. Used by permission.

Scripture quotations marked (NLT) are taken from the Holy Bible, New Living Translation, copyright © 1996, 2004, 2015 by Tyndale House Foundation. Used by permission of Tyndale House Publishers, Carol Stream, Illinois 60188, USA. All rights reserved.

Scripture taken from THE MESSAGE. Copyright © 1993, 1994, 1995, 1996, 2000, 2001, 2002. Used by permission of NavPress Publishing Group.

Scripture quotations marked (CEV) are taken from the CONTEMPORARY ENGLISH VERSION, Copyright© 1995 by the American Bible Society. Used by permission.

Scripture marked (ICB) are taken from the Holy Bible, International Children's Bible® Copyright© 1986, 1988, 1999, 2015 by Thomas Nelson. Used by permission. All rights reserved.

Scripture quotations marked (ISV) are taken from the INTERNATIONAL STANDARD VERSION, Copyright© 1996-2008 by the ISV Foundation. All rights reserved internationally.

Copyright © 2024 by Janelle Weeks
All rights reserved. No part of this book may be reproduced or stored in a retrieval system in any manner whatsoever without written permission except in the case of brief quotations embodied in reviews.

ISBN 979-8-218-56202-1

DEDICATION

This devotional is dedicated to all of my nieces and nephews. They provide so much vibrant color in my life. It is dedicated to Mark Harkins, the first to encourage me to share these stories in written form. And it is, of course, dedicated to my husband Dave. Always, always my very best friend, my cheerleader, and the nurturing cradle for my creativity.

Contents

	Winter – Darkest Valleys* 12
January	1.1 Becoming FAT – Dieting Tips, Part 1 15
	1.2 Staying FAT – Dieting Tips, Part 2 17
	1.3 Food Analogies – Dieting Tips, Part 3 19
	1.4 As Is 21
February	2.1 My Father's Hope 23
	2.2 ILYMTYLM 29
	2.3 Bum Calf and a 2x4 31
	2.4 Jump Frog 33
March	3.1 MaryJo, Joe, James 35
	3.2 Search for Diamonds – Vision, Part 1 37
	3.3 Skyscraper – Vision, Part 2 39
	3.4 Glory Story 41
	Spring – Salvation at Easter 46
April	4.1 Baby Chick 49
	4.2 Marigolds and Walnut Trees 51
	4.3 A Bit on Prayer – Prayer & Trust, Part 1 . . . 53
	4.4 A Bit on Trust – Prayer & Trust, Part 2 55
May	5.1 Prissy 57
	5.2 Snapshot of a Mother 59
	5.3 Lessons From Brandy 61
	5.4 Bouncing 63
June	6.1 I Love You 89 69
	6.2 When Life is Hard – Hope, Part 1 71
	6.3 Riding the Surfboard – Hope, Part 2 73
	6.4 Calming the Storm – Hope, Part 3 75

*52 stories but only 48 weeks, if each month is numbered as 4 weeks. And I wanted that, since many of my stories roughly match a holiday or certain time of year. So I dispersed the other 4 stories to represent each of the four seasons. Hope you can pace yourself!

	Summer – Marvelous Marinade 80
July	7.1 Norman 83
	7.2 A Well-Edited Life 85
	7.3 Galatians 2:20 87
	7.4 What You Don't Need 89
August	8.1 Here We Go a Waddling 95
	8.2 Good, Good Father – Identity, Part 1 97
	8.3 Pitch Your Tent – Identity, Part 2 99
	8.4 It Is Well 101
September	9.1 Solid Food 103
	9.2 A Jeep and a Blind Man 105
	9.3 Grandmother 107
	9.4 Cats, Cats, and More Cats 111
	Autumn – Rotten Tomatoes 116
October	10.1 Nine Ladies 119
	10.2 Paradox – Self-control/Stress, Part 1 . . . 121
	10.3 Quit Smoking – Self-control, Part 2 . . . 123
	10.4 Looking at Titus – Stress, Part 3 125
November	11.1 Not to Worry 127
	11.2 Aarons and Hurs 129
	11.3 Bringing Candy 131
	11.4 Receive the Bumps 133
December	12.1 Joy or Happiness? 139
	12.2 He Knows, He Cares – Sunsets, Part 1 . . 141
	12.3 Retirement Choices – Sunsets, Part 2 . . . 143
	12.4 Rain at Christmas 145
Leftovers:	Thinkin' About It 149
	Never Give Up 150
	Kip 153
	Hannah 155

Introduction

I talk too much. Everyone knows it and most people I'm around just put up with it. My husband has done so for several decades now, continually reassuring me that it's really not true. But we all know it is. I talk too much.

Every once in a while, however, somebody will respond positively to my verbiage and encourage me to continue. Usually, it's when I am telling a story. I love, love, love stories. I'm pretty sure others do also. I like analogies and remember-whens and real life examples and anecdotes and, well, …stories.

If you're a person who understands the imperative of connecting with God every day through prayer and Bible study, then you probably already know that a simple daily devotional book (like this one) is not adequate as the primary tool for growing that relationship. In our time alone with the Lord, He beckons us toward an in-depth, consistent perusal and meditation on His Word, as well as a regular, ongoing *time-on-your-knees* conversation with the Creator of the universe. And something I've realized over the years is that quite often the one day of the week most difficult to maintain my Quiet Time habit is on Sundays. Not sure why. Maybe it's the relaxed, weekend feel making me a little slow and lazy, or the subsequent pattern of rushing to get to church on time. Perhaps it's the excuse that connecting with my Maker in a corporate setting is surely good enough 52 days of the year. Whatever the reason, this devotional is an attempt to make the paths cross between my strength of sharing anecdotes and my weakness on Sunday mornings. If you're willing to walk that path with me, put an alert in your phone to remind you every week and carve out a few minutes to read a story.

Sunday Stories is a compilation of mostly random narratives, some funny, some serious, yet all of which have influenced my life and quite often through God's rebuke.

My hope is that they will make a mark on your life as well. Were I to choose a theme verse for this devotional that loosely encompasses the overall content, it would be Romans 12:12, where Paul reminds us to *"be joyful in hope, patient in affliction, faithful in prayer."* It is my desire to promote each of these things through my attempts at storytelling.

According to Proverbs 20:15, *"lips that speak knowledge are a rare jewel."* I really do try to be careful about what I say and when I say it. I have a desire for my spoken *jewels* to be more *rare* and less abundant. But to honor those who have encouraged me to write a devotional-style book, I now submit to you a few of my personal sentiments about life as a maturing Christ follower. And I must beg you not to heed Solomon's advice a few verses later in Proverbs 20, where he concludes that one should *"avoid a person who talks too much"* (v. 19). You can avoid me after you read. I promise to shut up at the end.

WINTER

*"Do your best to get here before **winter**…" – 2 Timothy 4:21*

The season of winter will sometimes bring us down. Whether it's the cold, the wind, loneliness over the holidays or maybe the shortened daylight hours, there could definitely be some disheartening moments that wreck us emotionally. This poem was written during one of those moments. But hope is not absent – it is simply waiting for us. Hope is persistent. It is patient. And as you work your way through these 52 stories, I believe you will find it a frequent and comforting companion.

WINTER MOURNING

the words do not come easy
this time

the poet within me is silent

I feel desperate
afraid

attempted a song even
the melody came
but not the words

in front of me an empty page
a perfect reflection
of the emptiness inside my heart

tell me
are the memories gone
or just the ability
to express them

such bitterness has settled in
an uninvited guest
it tangles with the emptiness
and signals a finality
I've never felt before

I can but wonder
as I am now trapped
within the depths
of this winter's cold embrace

will there be spring

Darkest Valleys

Take a moment. Breathe. Engage all of your senses and immerse yourself in the following:

You are sitting on a rock, warmed by the summer sun, in the middle of a peaceful mountain meadow. Smell the moist earth and wildflowers. Listen to the birds chirping, the breeze singing through surrounding trees, the water trickling over rocks in a nearby creek. Run your fingers through the tall grasses, feel the gentle wind on your face. Witness the greens and yellows of the aspen trees and evergreens at the edge of the field. Savor the beauty of God's creative handiwork.

Stand up. Lift your head and delight in the comforting caress of blue sky and bright sunlight. Walk slowly around this meadow. Take it all in. Revel in the tranquility of this place. Observe the majestic mountains beyond the aspens, rising up all around you. A mighty, shielding fortress – tall, blue, beautiful. Breathe deep. Feel the presence of the Creator. You are safe. Protected. Serene.

You do not leave. Slowly the day turns to dusk, then on into night. This darkened valley is still your secure anchor. Nothing has changed except your ability to see it. And where are you?

Psalm 23:4 says, *"though I walk through the <u>darkest valley</u>, I will fear no evil, for You are with me."* That quiet meadow is still there. Constant, unchanged, inhabited by the Almighty. In your darkest valleys, God remains. He has not moved. He surrounds you with splendor. Flowers, grass, birds, trees are as before, simply waiting for the sunrise to reveal their loyal stance. Do not fear. Bask in the reassuring knowledge that night is forever partnered with day. Sunlight, a devoted and trustworthy companion to darkness, will return. Engage your senses. Breathe the beautiful presence of God. Now. In the valley. In the darkness. The Lord is with you even when you cannot see.

Acts 27 recounts Paul's involuntary transport to Rome, with a violent storm and a shipwreck on an island. The ship is damaged and breaking apart. The prisoners, sailors and soldiers all endure raging seas, cargo tossed overboard, near starvation, and fear of imminent death. Paul urges them to take courage; he has been given a message from the Lord that all lives will be spared. The sailors apparently don't trust his claim. At night, they secretly try to escape in a lifeboat. Paul declares, *"unless these men stay with the ship, you cannot be saved"* (v. 31). They don't realize that fleeing will actually remove them from the one place where they are safe.

Paul's experience has relevance today. We all encounter dire conditions or turbulent storms in life that threaten our safety, health, freedom – sometimes our very lives. Such events can result in feelings of extreme anxiety, stress or depression. How do we respond? Out of desperation and fear, many of us react by attempting to solve those difficulties on our own. We throw out a "lifeboat" in an effort to escape the situation and feel more in control. But the lesson of this story is that our only safe choice is to remain in the place of refuge where God has promised protection. Proverbs 27:12 says, *"The prudent see danger and take refuge, but the simple keep going and pay the penalty."* We must learn to trust that God Himself is our safety. Our efforts to control only take us away from His assurance, His place of shelter and security.

The Lord never promised to remove us from storms or darkest valleys. In fact, for Paul, the darkness would last at least three more months. But twice in this passage, Paul tells the men to keep up their courage, trusting God to take care of them. Why would they need such courage? Because it would be a long time before they finally reached Rome. We too need to keep up our courage, trusting God to fulfill His promises. Sunlight is indeed coming to our darkest valleys, but it might just be awhile.

"If I say, 'Surely the darkness will overwhelm me, and the light around me will be night,' even darkness is not dark to You... darkness and light are alike to You." – Psalm 139:11-12 (NASB)

JANUARY

1.1

Dieting Tips, Part 1:
*How to Stay **F.A.T.** After the Holidays*

F*aithful.*

I think I have discovered a nearly revolutionary way of remaining faithful. It is called prayer. If you're like I was, you've heard of prayer and when you have some extra time you might even do it a little. But once I *tasted the fruits* of a consistent prayer life, I began to see its inevitable relationship to faithfulness.

Like most folks, I have a decent microwave (are you noticing my attempts to maintain a food theme?) that I have learned to appreciate and depend on for expediency and convenience in heating my food. One morning, I took my getting-cold coffee to a friend's house expecting to warm it in her microwave. She didn't have one! Impossible. How could anyone survive without?

My point is this: As I have learned to consistently appreciate and depend on a quality personal prayer time, I think - Impossible! How did I ever survive without? Praying daily helps me to be faithful in other things, faithful to the people in my life, and more faithful to Almighty God who increases my faith by honoring my prayers and, therefore, teaching me to be more… *faithful*.

A*vailable.*

The Bible reveals that there are basically just two things we are to major on and give our lives in exchange for: *people* and *the Word of God.* Not too much of a coincidence that these are the very same things which will last forever.

Matthew 6:33 states that we are to seek first the kingdom of God – which is *people* (Luke 17:21; Rev. 5:10), and His righteousness – which is *Christ/the Word* (1 Cor. 1:30, 2:16). True religion, according to James 1:27, means looking after the needs of *people* and staying unpolluted through resolute obedience to *God's Word*. If you give your life in exchange for these two things, you will be leaving a legacy that lasts forever.

Scripture encourages us to leave behind *people* as our inheritance (Deut. 32:9, Isa. 43:4). In order to do this, we must be... available! Now God does much to keep me busy, and I try my best to keep the word "too" in front of busy. I readily admit to a history of complaining about just how "too busy" I am. (There are some who might call this boasting.) But if my objective is to be available to people, am I not sabotaging my own goal by continually reminding everyone how busy I am?

This was made very clear to me once, through my early attempts at building a relationship with a non-Christian colleague. One Monday morning, she shared that she had spent her Friday night alone and bored. I glibly replied, "Hey, you should have called me. I wasn't doing anything either." My coworker then responded with this sad, but revealing accusation, "You? I would never think to call you. You're always way too busy."

I'm learning not to brag about how busy I am. It's a hard habit to break. But I want to be *available* for God's use by being perceived as such by the people He has put in my life.

I am excited to report that less than a year after this incident, I had learned enough about remaining available that God allowed me to be present when He welcomed this same friend into His saving arms of grace. God is so good, isn't He?

"A faithful person will be richly blessed..." – Proverbs 28:20

"He chose capable men from all over Israel and appointed them as leaders over the people... These men were always available..." – Exodus 18:25-26 (NLT)

"And arrange yourselves so that some of you will be available to help..." – 2 Chronicles 35:5 (GNT)

1.2

Dieting Tips, Part 2:
The Rest of the Story

***T**eachable.*
People often comment on how they just aren't being *fed* at their church, the sermons don't meet their needs, they aren't getting anything out of their community group, or their Bible study just isn't doing anything for them. I must say this rather irritates me. I am convinced that the truly teachable person can learn in just about any set of circumstances. I have found that if I'm listening, God will teach me amazing things all by Himself! I learn from people all the time, but I refuse to be dependent on others as the primary source for my spiritual food. I can be abundantly fed by the Creator alone, through meditating on His Word, praying, memorizing Scripture and listening to the Holy Spirit.

The teachable man King David recognized this in Psalm 119:102, where he proclaimed, *"I have not departed from Your laws, for You Yourself have taught me."* In Hebrews 5:14, we are told that *"solid food is for the mature, who by constant use have trained themselves to distinguish good from evil."* Take note that the mature aren't trained by someone else, but have *trained themselves* by constantly using the solid food of God's Word. There's that word "food" again - I just can't seem to get away from the dieting analogy! Well, maybe it's making you hungry (spiritually, of course). If you feed that hunger adequately, you might just end up getting F.A.T.

The opposite condition is actually mentioned in the Old Testament and is labeled *TEKEL*. It can be found in Daniel 5:27, where the writing on the wall revealed that Belshazzar had been weighed on the scales and found deficient. I guess he wasn't FAT enough for God's standards.

In this new year, I have two thoughts to add. The first came about because my husband showed me an article he had read, on how marriage can make you fat. It got me to thinking. Does my marriage make me FAT? If not, why not? Likewise, am I inspiring my husband to be more Faithful, Available and Teachable by my words, attitude, prayers and actions? Those of you who are married might want to resolve this year to pray specifically for *faithfulness, availability,* and *teachability* in yourself, your spouse, and your marriage. And if you are single, you could even be praying these qualities over your future spouse and marriage. Actually, all of us should also make the commitment to pray these same qualities into the marriages of other couples we know.

My second thought is tied to something I recently read, which added a couple of other words to the F.A.T. concept. The words were *Interested* and *Hungry*. We need to be both *interested in* and *hungry for* the things of God, or we will never stay FAT. Now if you try adding these words to the acronym, it actually creates the word FAITH. Hmmm... I sense a whole new essay brewing.

During my personal Bible reading on the morning after I finished writing this particular devotional message, I felt an unusual sense of prompting and anticipation from the Holy Spirit for what God might have to show me concerning this topic. Sure enough, I opened my Bible to the book of Isaiah, where I'd currently been studying in my Quiet Time, and began to read chapter ten. I actually laughed out loud.

Concerning the remnant of Israel, the Lord Almighty says that the survivors, who return to the Mighty God and truly rely on Him (in other words, those who remain *faithful, available,* and *teachable*), will have the yoke of the enemy broken and lifted from their shoulders *"because you have grown so FAT"* (Isa. 10:27). I am not kidding. It's in there. I rest my case.

"So you must remain faithful to what you have been taught from the beginning..." – 1 John 2:24 (NLT)

"The sovereign Lord... wakens my ear to listen like one being taught." – Isaiah 50:4

Dieting Tips, Part 3:
Random Thoughts on Staying Hungry

* *Hydrate often.* When someone habitually gets dehydrated, it's obvious they need healthier dietary habits. It is so very important to nurture frequently. We need a consistent, regular diet; one that is well balanced in good nutrition, has a variety of those beneficial vitamins, and includes lots of water! In the same way, a deprived and starving spirit is in need of Living Water and a consistent, healthy food source (i.e., daily time in the Word and in prayer).

* *It's a good thing to be hungry.* If your body never told you when it was hungry, you would become malnourished very quickly! Likewise, we all need the Holy Spirit to remind us of our spiritual hunger needs, so that we can stay in good shape. You probably know in order to make sourdough bread, you need what is called starter. Then you have to feed that starter on a regular basis or it will soon go bad. We must consistently feed our hunger. By this, I mean that we must develop a habit of making it grow, enticing and tantalizing that growth by feeding it more "yummy food" to digest (Jer. 15:16).

* *Don't bite off more than you can chew.* Now there's a helpful caution. Try digesting smaller portions – do not overdose on quantity and sacrifice quality. That is to say, take it slow whenever you are learning and exploring spiritual truths, and always try to go deeper in your studies. Hebrews 6:1 says that we should leave behind the elementary teachings and "*go on to maturity.*"

* *Become a Foodie.* A foodie is defined as someone with a keen, cultivated interest in food, eating not only out of hunger but also as a personal interest or hobby. These people are on a quest. They pursue good food with a great amount of zeal and eagerness. Hopefully it is *good food* they are pursuing – all those healthy vegetables and fruits! We ought to take up a passionate pursuit of our good God and the fruit He calls us to!

Have an ardent interest in knowing Him more, better, deeper. Refine your understanding of Jesus and the Holy Spirit; study the fruits of the Spirit. Then become an expert who can guide others to the deep truths of the gospel.

   * *Be your own food critic.* Why don't you try weighing yourself on the FAT measuring scale! In which of these areas might you need to gain a few pounds or change your diet --- Remaining Faithful? Being Available? Staying Teachable? Increasing your hunger? Maybe all of them? Even the most "in shape" person will tell you this is a daily, lifelong commitment and quite a safe distance from easy. But the benefits to your spiritual health will be incredible, very fulfilling and well worth your time. So set yourself a measurable, reachable goal and belly up to the table. *Delicious!*

   **One last thought for you to ponder as you go about your day: Do people who have made a habit of eating right, always enjoy every single bite? Or is it more probable that their satisfaction is necessarily tied to the results they begin to see over time? As you set about pondering, here are a few more "tasty" Scripture references you might want to study:

Job 23:12; Psalm 102:4; 119:103; 141:3-4; Isaiah 1:19; Ezekiel 2:8-3:3; John 4:31-34; 6:27, 35, 48-58; Acts 2:46-47; Revelation 10:9-10

1.4 ☙ ❧

As Is

We are traveling somewhere, my husband and I, sharing the back seat of a car and listening half-heartedly to the two in front as they continue a back-and-forth discussion about some folks they both know. I am watching out the window at the blur of grass and trees, and I hear the driver refer to one of those people as a "Has-been." Ouch! Not a very kind or flattering way to describe someone. And I think, not a very pleasant moniker for one to be known by. As the landscape continues to flash by outside, my thoughts continue to ponder this undignified title and I wonder if anyone has ever used such a phrase to describe me.

Leaning over to the man I love so much, I whisper, "Honey, do you think I'm a Has-been?"

Without hesitating, he quickly and adamantly whispers back, "No way, sweetie!" Short pause, then in a confident, serious and reassuring tone: "You're an *As Is!*"

I laugh out loud, a full belly laugh that startles the ones in front but somehow doesn't disrupt their dialogue. My good husband, who hands down loves me beyond measure, has a longstanding habit of accidentally saying things to me which are absurdly, ridiculously offensive. And each time I can do nothing but laugh, because he never means them the way they come out. Besides, when I really stop to think about it, isn't this exactly what I am?

Without a doubt, I have earned the credentials of an *As Is*. I come to Dave with all of my glaring flaws, my nature of sinfulness, my fast-approaching sell-by date, and yet seeing those many imperfections, he still accepts me, brings me in, promises to love me completely, unconditionally, for as long as we both shall live.

I remember a definition of Christian love I heard years ago. It has profoundly impacted my understanding of God-given intimacy and affection: *I will love you as you are, without requiring any promise of change on your part, or return for my love.* Our Heavenly Father does not wait for a good performance review. Because it's clear none of us could ever measure up. He offers His love, His personal and intimate relationship to all who realize they will never really deserve it. That it's not about cleaning up our act and earning a place at the table. That we must come as we are, with dirty feet only Christ can kneel to wash clean.

It is easy to see that Dave has already figured it out. He is choosing to love me as God has loved him. At the age of 26, this husband of mine watched in amazement when the Lord reached down and drew him to Himself, accepted him completely, loved him eternally, unconditionally – as is! – with all sins including future ones, forgiven at the Cross.

Our car drones on toward its destination, and I take note that there is now a glorious grin on the face reflected in my window. I reach over to grasp the hand of this imperfect man sitting next to me and squeeze three times, our silent and secret signal, my way of reciprocating his accidental message:
I. Love. You.

Then I add another trio of squeezes and I am hopeful that he gets it... *as. you. are.*

"But God demonstrates His own love for us in this: While we were still sinners, Christ died for us."
 – *Romans 5:8*

FEBRUARY 2.1

My father lived four months and two days past his eighty-first birthday. He lived passionately and determined, faithful and protective, full of wisdom, deep concern and fierce love. But he never lived as courageously or fully present as he did for the last year and a half that he was with us. I wrote the following just a couple of months before the Lord took His precious saint home.

My Father's Hope
"Precious in the sight of the Lord is the death of His saints."
– Psalm 116:15

    Yes, my dad is dying. We all are, really. But at age 81 and having cancer for the past year, my father is much more aware of this fact than most of us. I went to visit him recently after a downturn in his health, and experienced another God moment well worth the attempt at preserving with my inadequate words…

    I am at the kitchen table eating a breakfast of cold cereal and hot coffee, when my dad shuffles into the room and grabs my arm. "Come with me," he whispers. We head for the front door of his mountain home, which stands atop a canyon at the edge of the Big Horns. He pulls me out onto the front porch in my bare feet. It is early February. Pristine snow sparkles in the bright morning sun, as a slow breeze tickles my face and whispers through the evergreens in his front yard. The air is clean, yet the gentle wind brings with it a hint of pine needles and – how else to say it? – God's aroma of creation. My father scoots closer to the railing and motions me toward him. "Can you feel it?" he asks with intensity.

A pause. I wait quietly with expectation and growing curiosity. Another emotional whisper, "Can you feel it? Can you feel God's love?" More silence.

And then suddenly I can. As I stand there barefoot in the cold, in the quiet, I feel God's love in a new and unique way. I feel His creation with all my senses and I am completely overcome by the obvious presence of God's love for me, for my dad, for His people, for His world. When the tears begin to flow, I move closer and snake an arm around my father's frail body. We both hug and cry shamelessly, sharing the unusual sense that God is hugging us as well.

"I feel so blessed," my father says in a choked voice. "And yet, I feel so sad."

I think I know the reason, but I am wrong. "I feel so very sad because of all the years I missed out on this. God's love is so overwhelming to me that I feel I might burst with it. How could I have been so blind, so unaware? And I have denied God the many years of deep praise He deserves for all that He does to bring us joy in this world."

We stand a few minutes more and enjoy the silence together. I strain to drink in the morning, to memorize the sights and sounds and smells. He squeezes me tightly and says, "Well, I'm sorry your cereal's probably soggy. But I had to bring you out here while the temperature was right because I knew He was waiting for us."

Isn't God always waiting for us? Waiting for us to stop the busyness and the lists and the rat race and the day-to-day and the excuses and the distractions? *"Come to Me, all you who are weary and burdened, and I will give you rest"* (Mt. 11:28). Scripture tells us in James 4:14 that our life is like a mist, that appears for a little while and then vanishes. We just need to be willing to let the coffee get cold and take a moment to rest in God's loving presence.

This is my father's hope. This is my *Father's* hope. It is becoming mine also. I hope.

* I'd like to give you an opportunity at this point to journal your thinking. Have you lost someone close to you who played a role in who you are today? Try writing your memories about that experience. Or maybe choose a verse about hope or love or both, and share your thoughts on that passage of Scripture. Or do you have a favorite song on this topic? Write out the lyrics or create your own poetry:

Well, here we are. It's that time of year again… time to observe Valentine's Day. Send cards. Buy roses. Talk about love. Eat a few chocolates. Celebrate with a sweetheart. Some people love it – some people dread it. But God had a different intent when He introduced us to the reality of love. His love. There's no getting around it. We are all commanded to LOVE one another. Almost 40 times in the New Testament this concept is addressed. How would you define it? What notable traits does God-given love display? How does it uniquely express itself?

WHAT *IS* LOVE?

I used to know exactly what **love** is
...before I met YOU...

It was simple and didn't demand much;

It was *want* and like

self and *fantasy*

infatuation, *greed* –

It was *ME*.

Now I am much confused, you see
... since I met YOU...

What is this thing that pushed aside **love**?

It isn't simple and demands much;

It is *commitment* and need

selflessness and *reality*

complete joy, *constant fulfillment* –

It is *YOU*.

2.2

ILYMTYLM

When one of my nieces was about five, she created a telephone game that she loved to play with all aunts, uncles and grandparents. First, she would beg her mother to let her call and talk to us. Then she'd get on the phone and chitchat for a while about five-year-old things. After a bit, her manner would suddenly change and she'd begin her extended exit ritual of asking, "Are you done talking yet?" We always knew what was coming, so we would often try to keep her engaged and conversing until she started to get impatient and her voice sounded somewhat irritated.

Whenever the answer to her question was finally a surrendering yes, she would quickly respond by proudly proclaiming, "I LOVE YOU MORE THAN YOU LOVE ME!", as fast and as loud as she could. As you might predict, this was immediately followed by the pre-planned action of hanging up the phone before we had time to respond. It was definitely cute and clever.

In fact, my husband and I both thought it was so cute and clever that we decided to carry on this tradition by playing a similar game of our own. We've shortened the message a little and we don't hang up on the other one. But we do often sign our cards and notes with the acronym ILYMTYLM. We send it in our personal emails and frequently text it to each other. Sometimes we even get a bit competitive and add a few extra letters, such as IL**Y**WMTY**CE**LM, to see if the other can figure out what it stands for (this extended acronym, if you haven't guessed, means "I love you **way** more than you **could ever** love me"). We also like to argue about it, playfully giving various reasons to prove that we are the one who loves the other significantly more. Oh, so very silly and juvenile.

Why do we do it? Well, even though it may seem rather shallow and ridiculous, perhaps there is an underlying deeper intent. Scripture assures us repeatedly that God has lavished

His unique and perfect love on us. He demonstrated that unimaginable love through the sacrificial death of His Son Jesus on a cross, knowing that we would never be able to return His love as it was given.

Perfect. Untainted by our humanness.

But isn't it conceivable that along with God's gift of abundant, impossible-to-compete-with love toward us, there comes a desire, a longing to do the same? To give out more love than we could ever get in return? To imitate and express such a love to those whom God has placed in our lives? Perhaps my husband and I are simply recognizing, on some subconscious level, the need to love one another in an unreturnable way – just as Christ has loved us.

I submit this to you: My husband *does* love me more than I love him... but, I also love him more than he loves me! We are able to do this only through God's extravagant love gifted to each of us, a love with the power to reach beyond what could ever be given back.

"As I have loved you, so you must love one another."
    – John 13:34b

"...have sincere love for each other, love one another deeply, from the heart." – 1 Peter 1:22

"Dear friends, let us love one another, for love comes from God... since God so loved us, we also ought to love one another." – 1 John 4:7, 11

2.3

Bum Calf and a 2x4

Seems like it happened every year. Maybe not, but definitely often enough to be burned in my childhood memories. My family raised cattle. Every spring, of course, they all had babies. Most years we had a good chunk of cows that were heifers, giving birth for the first time. And frequently this resulted in a difficult delivery. It wasn't always pretty.

One year we had a mama who lost her calf during that process. At the same time, her hind legs became paralyzed. This happened more than once during my growing up years. We had this winch apparatus that we would use to try and get the paralyzed heifer walking. It was an iron vice that tightened around the cow's hips and hoisted her up so she could rest her back hooves on the ground. This allowed her to move around a little, and over several weeks of lifting multiple times a day, the heifer would often regain feeling and full movement. Plus, it let the newborn calf feed on mama's milk.

It so happened there was also a bum calf in the herd while the winch treatment was going on that spring. My father came up with the idea to put the two together. A paralyzed cow with no baby and a newborn with no food supply. That hungry calf was definitely willing to get his milk from any source, but the heifer did not take a shine to some young foreigner attacking her udder. So my dad took a 2x4 plank and when the cow tried to move away from the calf, he hit her with it. I don't suppose it felt too good, and she soon got the message to stand still. It was a twice daily ritual. Both animals became so conditioned to it that whenever they saw my dad head to the corral brandishing his 2x4, stubborn mama cow stood still and adorable baby cow raced over to the milk dispenser. We continued this procedure even after the heifer had returned to full mobility, hoping she would eventually accept the calf as her own.

Finally, my dad said enough. If that cow was not going to tolerate her new stepchild, then tough. He was done trying.

Time to send the pair back to the herd and see what happened. We were all praying for a miracle as we opened the corral gate that day. We watched our negligent heifer take off at a trot in newfound freedom, heading up the hill toward the pasture.

Alone. The poor calf just stayed in the corral, bawling and bleating and abandoned. It was so sad to watch. But it wasn't what made us cry. At the top of the rise, the heifer suddenly stopped and turned. A reluctant mama's moo finally resonated, beckoning the lonely little calf to lope up that hill and join his newly adopted family. Now *we* were the ones bawling.

God heard our petitions that day. It was a miracle, no doubt in our minds. But it was a Scripture lesson as well, about the cattle on a thousand hills, about one lost sheep who matters more, about the birds of the air who are cared for and fed by their loving Father. A radical Father Who assures us that He values *us* even more.

"Every animal of the forest is already Mine. The cattle on a thousand hills are Mine." – Psalm 50:10, ICB

"If a man owns a hundred sheep, and one of them wanders away, will he not…go to look for the one…? And if he finds it, truly I tell you, he is happier about that one sheep than about the ninety-nine that did not wander off." – Matthew 18:12-13

"Look at the birds of the air; they do not sow or reap or store away in barns, and yet your heavenly Father feeds them. Are you not much more valuable than they?" – Matthew 6:26

"But you who revere My name… will go out and frolic like well-fed calves." – Malachi 4:2

2.4

Jump Frog

Maybe you've heard the old joke that goes something like this:

A research scientist took a frog and set it on the ground. He said, "Jump, frog, jump!" And the frog jumped 6 feet. The scientist took out his little notebook and wrote, *4 feet – 6 feet.* Then he cut off one of the frog's legs and said, "Jump, frog, jump!" The frog jumped 4 feet. The scientist wrote in his notebook, *3 feet – 4 feet.* Then he cut off another of the frog's legs and said, "Jump, frog, jump!" This time the frog jumped 2 feet. So the scientist wrote, *2 feet – 2 feet.* He cut off the third leg and again said, "Jump, frog, jump!" The frog only jumped 6 inches. And the scientist wrote, *1 foot – ½ a foot.* Finally, he cut off the last leg and said, "Jump, frog, jump!" The frog just sat there. He said it louder, "Jump, frog, jump!" Still the frog didn't move. The scientist shouted once more, "Jump, frog, jump!" No movement. So he took out his little notebook one final time and wrote, *no feet - frog turns deaf.*

Now that's just silly. About as silly as a lot of people I know, maybe even including myself now and then. We go through life making poor decision after poor decision and then cry out, "Help, God, help!" And He does. He guides us to Scripture. He provides people who listen and care and understand and share their wisdom. He shows us the right path. He intervenes. He speaks to us through the Holy Spirit. He helps.

But how often do we simply return to the same awful mistakes or bow down to the same worthless idols? Choices we know from experience and training not to make, yet we do. Then we cry out again, "Help, God, help!" And again, God hears and heeds and helps and heals. But the negative patterns continue until the consequences seem intolerable. At last, our miserable cries result in silence. Then, unbelievably, we come to the scientist's ridiculous conclusion: God must be deaf. Why doesn't He hear me? Why isn't He answering my cry for help? God must not care.

Our arrogant, inaccurate assumption that God has turned a deaf ear, reveals our ignorance. The Lord does indeed care. He has already given us every possible thing we might need for life and godliness, through our knowledge of Him Who called us by His own glory and goodness (2 Pet. 1:3). He has already accomplished immeasurably more than all we could ever ask or imagine, and this according to His supernatural power which is always at work within us (Eph. 3:20).

It's time to stop being silly. To sacrifice our habits, hurts and hang ups at the altar of repentance and choose to live in the salvation life that is *already* ours.

"You brought my life up from the pit, O Lord my God. When my life was ebbing away, I remembered You, Lord, and my prayer rose to You, to Your holy temple. Those who cling to worthless idols turn away from God's love for them. But I, with shouts of grateful praise, will sacrifice to You. What I have vowed I will make good. Salvation comes from the Lord." – Jonah 2:6b-9

2.4

Jump Frog

Maybe you've heard the old joke that goes something like this:

A research scientist took a frog and set it on the ground. He said, "Jump, frog, jump!" And the frog jumped 6 feet. The scientist took out his little notebook and wrote, *4 feet – 6 feet.* Then he cut off one of the frog's legs and said, "Jump, frog, jump!" The frog jumped 4 feet. The scientist wrote in his notebook, *3 feet – 4 feet.* Then he cut off another of the frog's legs and said, "Jump, frog, jump!" This time the frog jumped 2 feet. So the scientist wrote, *2 feet – 2 feet.* He cut off the third leg and again said, "Jump, frog, jump!" The frog only jumped 6 inches. And the scientist wrote, *1 foot – ½ a foot.* Finally, he cut off the last leg and said, "Jump, frog, jump!" The frog just sat there. He said it louder, "Jump, frog, jump!" Still the frog didn't move. The scientist shouted once more, "Jump, frog, jump!" No movement. So he took out his little notebook one final time and wrote, *no feet - frog turns deaf.*

Now that's just silly. About as silly as a lot of people I know, maybe even including myself now and then. We go through life making poor decision after poor decision and then cry out, "Help, God, help!" And He does. He guides us to Scripture. He provides people who listen and care and understand and share their wisdom. He shows us the right path. He intervenes. He speaks to us through the Holy Spirit. He helps.

But how often do we simply return to the same awful mistakes or bow down to the same worthless idols? Choices we know from experience and training not to make, yet we do. Then we cry out again, "Help, God, help!" And again, God hears and heeds and helps and heals. But the negative patterns continue until the consequences seem intolerable. At last, our miserable cries result in silence. Then, unbelievably, we come to the scientist's ridiculous conclusion: God must be deaf. Why doesn't He hear me? Why isn't He answering my cry for help? God must not care.

Our arrogant, inaccurate assumption that God has turned a deaf ear, reveals our ignorance. The Lord does indeed care. He has already given us every possible thing we might need for life and godliness, through our knowledge of Him Who called us by His own glory and goodness (2 Pet. 1:3). He has already accomplished immeasurably more than all we could ever ask or imagine, and this according to His supernatural power which is always at work within us (Eph. 3:20).

It's time to stop being silly. To sacrifice our habits, hurts and hang ups at the altar of repentance and choose to live in the salvation life that is *already* ours.

"You brought my life up from the pit, O Lord my God. When my life was ebbing away, I remembered You, Lord, and my prayer rose to You, to Your holy temple. Those who cling to worthless idols turn away from God's love for them. But I, with shouts of grateful praise, will sacrifice to You. What I have vowed I will make good. Salvation comes from the Lord." – Jonah 2:6b-9

MARCH 3.1

MaryJo, Joe, James

When I was in college, one of the first girls I ever discipled was a freshman on my dorm floor. I'm pretty sure I learned more from MaryJo than she ever learned from me. She was young, naïve, and had a simple faith which led her into a habit of praying about everything.

On a dreary Saturday afternoon, I was feeling rather lonely and discouraged. So I headed down the hall to MaryJo's room to vent about my depressed and solitary woes.

Her advice? "You should pray and ask God to have Joe call you." Uh-oh. Time for the teacher to impart wisdom to her pupil.

Joe was a guy I had a crush on. He didn't, however, have a crush on me. We had dated for a very short time a few months back, and now our relationship consisted of him being friendly whenever we happened to see each other or if I decided to call him. But that was it. Joe never called me. Ever.

"Listen MaryJo, I cannot do that. You see, my motives would be really selfish and the Bible tells us in the book of James that we shouldn't pray and ask with wrong motives. If I'm feeling lonely, I can just talk to God Himself. I don't need to be asking the Lord to have some boy call me. It wouldn't be right."

There. Life on life discipleship at its finest.

MaryJo just looked at me and smiled. "You know, I think sometimes God answers prayers simply because He wants to and not always because it's the right kind of prayer."

I tried to form an instructive response. But, really, how do you reply to that? So I just said, "Well I can't do it." And then I headed back down the hall to my dorm room, muttering to myself and mentally stomping the whole way.

About five minutes later my phone rang. It was Joe. Really, it was. "Hey there, I was just calling to see how you're doing since I haven't heard from you in a while." We chatted for a bit about this and that, just catching up. After the conversation ended, I hung up and immediately started a new one with my Father.

Okay, Lord, that was weird. What's going on here? What are You trying to teach me? I know I was right about the James verse and my motives, so I really don't get it.

Look it up. Twice He said it. *Look it up.*

So I looked it up. James 4:3 says, *"When you ask, you do not receive, because you ask with wrong motives, that you may spend what you get on your pleasures."*

See there, Lord, it says not to ask when you have the wrong motives! *Read it again.* So I did. And on about the third reading, I finally paid attention to the very first word.

When. God never said don't ask. He said **when** you ask. You are not called to be the editor of your own prayer life. This is the Holy Spirit's job (Rom. 8:26-27). You can ask the Lord for anything. If you don't receive what you asked for, you might want to consider whether your reasons for asking were selfish. But the bottom line is, stop editing your prayers and start working on your motives.

"...We do not know what we ought to pray for, but the Spirit himself intercedes for us through wordless groans."
                                         – Romans 8:26

3.2 ଔ ଓ

Vision, Part 1: *Searching for Diamonds*

There's an old tale that goes like this: *Once upon a time, there was a small village deep within a valley, completely surrounded by steep and towering mountains. At night by the fire, a legend was told of an enormous and beautiful diamond nestled atop one of the high, distant peaks. Many a man had attempted to climb those perilous cliffs and retrieve that glorious diamond. But the way was treacherous and steep, with a distance clearly demanding years of commitment, and none of the treasure hunters had ever returned.*

One day, another brave young lad proclaimed to those in the village, his bold resolve to summit this far away mountain peak. So great was his desire to own such a precious diamond that he would sacrifice much of his life to bring it back.

Off he set on his quest up the path, through the trees, over boulders, with many falls and scrapes and cuts and pains, and all the while fighting off a myriad of dangerous, wild animals and unpredictable mountain weather changes. The man trudged and climbed and aged and persevered. At last, many years later, he dragged and scraped his way over the top of the very highest cliff.

He had made it! Now, at a much slower pace than the start of his journey, the man desperately hobbled around, hunting everywhere for his long-awaited prize – that priceless, coveted diamond. He could not find the treasured stone. After days of frantic searching, he finally abandoned hope and slumped to the ground in defeat, his weary and beaten body crushed in the realization that he had just given his entire life for a myth.

Then quite unexpectedly, as he lay there mourning his failure and his fate, the old man noticed something shining brightly off in the distance through the trees. He leaned forward, squinting anxiously. There, far away on the opposite peak, lay the glimmering diamond he had so desired – a very real and valuable treasure that now would never be his. Sadly, this poor fellow had committed his entire life to climbing the wrong mountain. The End

Alright, I confess. I made up that story. But perhaps you've been told a similar one about somebody who needs to climb a high wall in order to reach freedom on the other side. He leans his ladder against the wall and climbs to the top, only to realize in the end that he has placed his ladder against the wrong wall. There's no escape from that direction and all of his efforts have been in vain, all his time spent for naught.

The question becomes, what if you gain a perspective and vision for what you want to gain in life, and you run with it – only to find at the end you were running on the wrong path? That you had leaned your life's ladder against the wrong wall?

D.L. Moody once said, "Our greatest fear should not be that of failure, but of succeeding at something which doesn't really matter." The only guidebook worth studying, to ensure you are running in the right direction, is the Bible itself. Commit to a habit of daily time spent delving deep into God's Word – hearing, reading, studying, memorizing, meditating, and asking the Holy Spirit to guide you in applying Scripture to all of your decisions and actions. Don't lean your ladder against a wall that isn't worth it. There will be unavoidable, eternally significant consequences.

Paul cautioned the believers in Corinth to *"run in such a way as to get the prize"* (1 Cor. 9:24). Be certain that all of your initiative, your vision and efforts are sending you up the mountain that actually has the treasure!

"…let us run with perseverance the race marked out for us."
– Hebrews 12:1

"…I press on toward the goal to win the prize for which God has called me heavenward in Christ Jesus." – Philippians 3:14

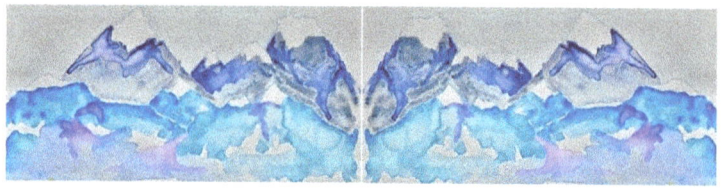

Vision, Part 2: *Gaining Focus*

Question: How do we gain vision and grow in it, obtaining the right spiritual focus and direction? Well, it definitely doesn't happen overnight. Psalm 37:4 says, *"Delight yourself in the Lord, and He will give you the desires of your heart."* I have found that most people tend to mumble right past the first half of this verse to emphasize the part about gaining the desires of our hearts. We all want to realize our heart desires and dreams, but the only way to truly gain those is to live out the first half of the verse.

If you stand in the lobby of a skyscraper and look out the window, all that you'll be able to see is possibly another lobby window across the street. Your vision is limited. But if you get in the elevator and go up several floors, you will be able to see that whole street and maybe even observe the roofs of some shorter buildings. Ride up a few more stories, and you'll likely see beyond several more streets, maybe spot a nearby park or neighborhood. Take that elevator to the top of the skyscraper and you will finally capture the entire city from all directions. Your perspective has changed significantly from when you were on the ground floor.

The analogy here is that with significant time in the ascending elevator, your vision for the city grows and you begin to see the bigger picture. Similarly, if you spend considerable time *delighting yourself in the Lord*, via Scripture intake and prayer, it changes what your heart desires. You will long for what is on God's heart as you gain His perspective and vision for the world. So the verse noted above is certainly accurate, because time spent delighting in the Lord yields heart desires that align with His. If you need confirmation, look at the two verses this statement is sandwiched in between: *"trust in the Lord"* (v. 3) and *"commit your way to the Lord"* (v. 5). Our heart yearnings and desires will line up with God's when we learn to trust Him and commit our lives to Him.

Another way to pose the question about vision and focus is *how do we get on the heavenly elevator?* In Luke 10:41-42, after Martha complains that Mary is not assisting with the preparations, Jesus corrects her by saying, *"you are worried and upset about many things, but only one thing is needed."* It is so easy to become bothered and hung up on desires that do not matter. When we choose to sweat the small stuff, allowing ourselves to get quickly sidetracked and distracted by potential stressors, we find ourselves missing that one necessary thing. *We should be sitting at the feet of Jesus, absorbing His Words, delighting in that intimate relationship.* Nothing else matters. Nothing else is ever worth fretting over.

Start today. Spend some quality time with God, exploring His Holy Word, praying and listening to the Spirit. Ask Him to guide you and show you how to trust, to commit your ways to Him. Meditate on the helpful verses listed below. You need to actively pursue gaining that vision *now*. Don't talk yourself into putting it off and working on it later. It surely gets no easier when you delay. And if you're convinced that you can just wait awhile to figure out which elevator to ride up, you are fooling yourself – you have already leaned your "life ladder" firmly against the wrong wall; the wall of procrastination.

"Where there is no vision, the people are unrestrained"
– Proverbs 29:18a (NASB)

"Son of man, look with your eyes and hear with your ears and pay attention to everything I am going to show you, for that is why you have been brought here…" *– Ezekiel 40:4*

3.4

What is your Glory Story?

God is always at work writing stories in our lives that will be for His glory. As you can tell, I love to share anecdotes about the things God has done in my life to draw attention to Himself. But *you* have stories too. The Lord has woven amazing miracles into every person's life. Recounting those tales can bring Him further praise and adoration, as others rejoice in His goodness. There is glory in the telling. So let me encourage you to give the Heavenly Father His high place of praise through your stories. Here is one of mine:

I made many trips to Laramie when I was young and single. My sister lived there, so I would visit her often. I had a Pontiac Grand Prix in those days. It served me well for several years, taking me to grad school in Indiana, packed full of everything I owned. Then bringing me back 2 years later with a master's degree and about the same load of belongings. My car lasted a few more years until I had an involuntary trade-in at the corner of 12th and Beech in my new hometown of Casper, Wyoming. I can truthfully say it wasn't my fault, but this didn't change the fact that my beloved car was now totaled. My glory story, however, took place before the eventual demise of this vehicle.

The frequent trips to see my sister began as soon I returned from Indiana. Because I was young and dumb and oblivious to the potential dangers of traveling alone, I often chose to make the return trip home very late in the evening. It was a two-and-a-half-hour drive over some pretty desolate roads. On one such night, I became acutely aware of my vulnerability when I experienced a blowout on one of my tires. There was an abrupt booming-type noise as my car started to shimmy and rattle, becoming suddenly very difficult to steer. Oh no. I heard the flapping sound of loose rubber on asphalt and knew exactly what had happened. There was fear in my heart as I braked and maneuvered to the shoulder. I just sat there shaking and crying. I was alone late at night in the middle of nowhere and

I barely knew how to change a flat tire. All I had was a donut spare and there were still about sixty miles of road ahead. It was cold, windy and very dark. I cried some more and prayed out loud, begging the Lord to please help me. I sat this way for several minutes, imploring my God to intervene somehow – to rescue His foolish, imprudent child and miraculously produce a Good Samaritan on this isolated stretch of highway.

No one came. Eventually, I dried my eyes and grabbed a flashlight from the glove box. That tire wasn't going to change itself. Braving the biting wind, I exited the car and shined my light at the front tire I thought was flat. Nope, it was fine.

Slightly puzzled, I moved to the next and then to each of the rear tires, but none of them looked flat. I checked each one again. All four were perfect and round and beautiful and impossible, and I immediately began crying again. I sat in my car for a long time, praising the Lord and then conversely worrying that somehow I was wrong. Was it really imaginable that I was seeing a miracle of God? Could I trust Him enough to actually drive the rest of the way home? Turns out I could.

I shared my miracle story with my Sunday School class the next morning and believe it or not, had a friend from the group approach me later and berate me for calling it a miracle. He said I was probably imagining it and making too big a deal out of it; that it certainly wasn't God "healing" my tire.

Wow. Can I just ask you to be careful how you respond to someone else's glory story? Even in your private, skeptical heart of hearts, don't ever doubt God's miracles. Don't be that person. The Lord chose to shine His love and grace in an extraordinary way that night, and He allowed me to be the one blessed by it. *To God be the glory, great things He has done!*

"Let the redeemed of the Lord tell their story…" – Psalm 107:2

"All this is for your benefit, so that the grace that is reaching more and more people may cause thanksgiving to overflow to the glory of God." – 2 Corinthians 4:15

"…the Lord will be your everlasting light, and your God will be your glory." – Isaiah 60:19

Notes on this past season…
* What has God been teaching you?
* Do you have a glory story you need to write down?

SPRING

*"Let us acknowledge the LORD, let us press on to acknowledge Him... He will come to us... like the **spring** rains that water the earth." – Hosea 6:3*

When our attention is drawn to thoughts of this coming season, we might find ourselves pondering new beginnings. Warmer weather. Enjoying the outdoors once again. God's new creation rising up from the earth while moisture pours down from above. I must admit that His gift of rain-drenched, flowering beauty inspires me and I simply have to compose a response.

She loves the rain

As the huge ball of orange sun
teases its way down the western side of an April sky,
spreading vibrant colors along the edge of the horizon,
a tremendous gray-blue storm cloud asserts itself into the picture.
God's unique sprinkler system goes to work
on this particular section of earth
as thousands upon thousands of raindrops fall from the cloud.

She runs quickly out into the yard
Warm wet splashes land on an upturned face,
trace the length of an eyebrow,
follow the contours of a smiling face
or run down the bridge of her nose to hesitate briefly
before plunging into the soft green grass below.

She is in her own private world
The rain makes pit-pat noises on the yellow plastic of her raincoat
while nose and mind concentrate together,
trying to preserve the fresh damp smell
within the walls of her memory.
Low laughter bubbles up and out into the crisp, clean air
as the Creator slowly veils His sun's majestic colors
behind the distant purple mountains,
turning day gently into night.

I am she

⊰ ⊱
Salvation at Easter

When he married me, my husband inherited a passel of nieces and nephews. Three already by our wedding date and another two not long after. A trio of daughters belonged to my brother, whereas my sister had one of each. All five of them, I am blessed to say, have a personal relationship with their Lord and Savior Jesus Christ. And it has been my distinct pleasure to be present when several of them began that journey of faith.

My oldest niece was only four when she heard me talking about the gospel message with a couple of friends after dinner one night. "I wanna do that!" she said to me. Not convinced that she fully understood, I started over, using a method called The Wordless Book, which conveys the gospel simply using colors. She was perched on my lap at the dining room table, so I grabbed nearby items to explain. Yellow mustard to represent the streets of gold and the perfection of heaven. A pepper shaker became the dark color, symbolizing how sin in each of us creates a separation from God. I pulled over the ketchup bottle and shared how Christ's blood, shed on the cross, made a way for us as He took the ultimate punishment for our sins. Salt was my visual to describe the washing clean that occurs in us when we admit our sin and accept God's free gift of eternal life through His Son. My niece did indeed understand and prayed right there to become a child of God. She proceeded to inform my sister, "Guess what, mommy? I'm Jesus's kid!"

A couple of years later, we went on a camping trip with my brother's family, up near Laramie Peak in southeast Wyoming. On a warm and sunny August morning, sitting in a tent with her aunt, my brother's oldest prayed a surrendering prayer of salvation at the tender age of five. Such joy.

Fast forward another few years. During family visits to see my young nieces and nephew, I had made a habit of always tucking each of them in at night, telling a fun bedtime story, and then praying together. On one such occasion, my youngest niece started peppering me with questions. Her inquisitive seven-year-old mind wanted to comprehend more about God, the Bible, Jesus. I shared the same Wordless Book gospel story I had explained to her cousin several years before.

"Megan, is this something you want to pray about right now?" She certainly did. After praying a beautiful confession, and relinquishing herself to accept God's precious gift of life in His Son Jesus, my niece made an enthusiastic proclamation.

"I can't wait till my birthday!"

I should note here that this was the middle of March. Megan's birthday was less than a month away. I was so disappointed. Obviously, she didn't get it. Her prayer had apparently been more my words than hers, and she was not ready or mature enough to fully grasp the message of the gospel.

So I smiled and said, "I bet you're looking forward to it."

"Yes, because my birthday is on Easter this year!"

There it was. My brilliant niece had figured out that she would have the unique opportunity of celebrating both her physical birthday and her spiritual birthday alongside the celebration of Christ's *re*birth day – conquering death and the grave – a resurrected and living Savior. Hallelujah!

Jesus said to her, "I am the resurrection and the life. Whoever believes in Me, though he die yet shall he live."
  – John 11:25 (ESV)

APRIL 4.1
Baby Chick

"...we also rejoice in our sufferings, because we know that suffering produces perseverance; perseverance, character; and character, hope. And hope does not disappoint..." – Rom. 5:3-5

These were some of the first Bible verses I committed to memory in college. Sophomore year was a significant time period in my growth spiritually, after the world had slowly gotten a stronghold in many areas of my life. The Lord was definitely *not* my top priority at the time, but I wasn't able to see it. He began to strip me of those things which had become so sadly important, taking away the distractions that I was allowing to guide many of my choices. One result of this purging was a sudden, clear awareness of the emptiness within me. It was a time of heavy darkness and oppression; I was certainly not a joyful person inside. But even as He removed these worldly enticements, God was filling me with the comfort of His Word.

A defining moment came when I was drawn to a statement at the end of Romans 5:2 and then kept reading. *"We rejoice in the hope of the glory of God..."* Not only so, but I can rejoice in *suffering* as well. Wow! Suffering produces perseverance, teaches character, and results in hope. All my discouragement, frustration and suffering over the things of this world were not to be despised, but rejoiced over! Why? Because they were all valuable and useful tools for producing godly character in me, when shaped by the power of the Holy Spirit.

Back when I was in junior high, my Sunday School teacher told us about an incident that had happened on their farm. Apparently, her young son had gone into the hen house one day and noticed a baby chick in the process of trying to break out of its eggshell. Feeling sorry for the young bird and the obvious difficulty it was encountering, he began to peel the shell apart in an effort to lessen its suffering circumstance.

You may be surprised to learn that the chick lived. But for what remained of its life, that chicken walked around with its head lolling to the side. It was not able to hold its neck and head erect because the necessary muscles had never developed properly during the difficult hatching process. All baby birds must endure this early struggle, in order to have the strength needed to make it through life with their heads "held high."

At the risk of overdoing it with analogies, I must also share something I learned while touring the vineyards of Napa Valley several years ago. The grape vines are nurtured with plenty of water in the early stages of growth, to establish and encourage a strong root system and foundation. As they mature and begin to produce fruit, however, they are given very little water. This amount is decreased purposefully, so that the vine's roots have to struggle to find their nourishment. In the long run, making the water source difficult to locate is best for the vine's stability and for the fruit as well. Too much water causes the grapes to become diluted and therefore much less valuable as an end-product.

Psalm 119:71 says, *"It was good for me to be afflicted, so that I might learn Your decrees."* The point worth reflecting on is that those arduous and painful things which generate such unbelievable chaos in our lives, are the very same things that can prepare us as believers to grow strong in our faith. We are to rejoice not only in good things, but in our sufferings as well – those wretched, miserable stressors that try so hard to ruin us – because they bring about the perseverance necessary for genuine character growth and sustaining hope. And it's because of such hope that we do not need to worry about the potential of future disappointments! At the end of Romans 5:5, we are also promised the supreme pleasure and nourishing satisfaction of God's perfect love poured out and overflowing in our hearts through His Holy Spirit.

Amen and amen!

"No discipline seems pleasant at the time, but painful. Later on, however, it produces a harvest of righteousness and peace for those who have been trained by it." – Hebrews 12:11

4.2

Marigolds and Walnut Trees

A few years back, one of my coworkers handed me an education article to read entitled "Find Your Marigold" (J. Gonzalez, 2013). It got me to thinking.

There is such a thing as *companion planting*. In gardening and agriculture, different crops are planted in close proximity to each other for several purposes. Companion plants will increase crop productivity by improving pest control and pollination, and they provide a habitat which entices beneficial creatures. In other words, if you place certain crops near others, it will advance their growth. Did you know that planting garlic next to your roses will help prevent fungal disease? And vine growers often plant roses beside their grapes as an early alert to bugs and weather changes.

Marigolds are prime examples, and one of the greatest companion plants available. They shield other plants from a variety of harmful insects and weeds, and they also repel another, much larger plant predator – deer. Put marigolds by your backyard garden vegetables and they will become stronger, healthier, longer-lasting plants.

Is it possible that God is using nature, His creation, as a perfect example for how we relate to those in our own life's *backyard*? I believe we need to look for and stay close to all of the "marigolds" the Lord places in our lives. If we are intentional about this, we will certainly grow and flourish and thrive where He has planted us.

Better yet, BE a marigold! Intentionally seek to encourage others, nourish their growth, and challenge those within your sphere of influence to become their very best. Practice the biblical traits of helping, supporting, serving, motivating, and loving. Be the kind of person others will want to be around.

Be warned, however, that knowledgeable, productive gardeners never put their vegetables next to walnut trees. This is because walnut trees discharge a noxious substance that hinders growth. Nearby plants easily wither and eventually die. The lesson here is obvious. Be careful how often you hang out with "walnut trees" – those toxic and cancerous people which you are likely to encounter in almost any circle. There is a high likelihood you will be poisoned by their attitude. Stay far away (Rom. 16:17), except in those situations where the Lord is obviously leading you to be a godly influence.

Most importantly, never choose to be a walnut tree. There are certain qualities you might look for as warning signs that you have joined this poisonous grove. Toxic people will often be arrogant, self-focused, negative, hateful, whiny, shallow, unwilling to submit to authority, impersonal, full of gossip, or lacking a servant heart. Do any of those traits sound like you?

If you read Psalm 1:1-3, I think you will notice a very similar analogy for this Marigold and Walnut Tree principle, in the clear caution never to plant yourself next to the wicked. Instead, there is blessing in being a tree which daily delights in obedience to the Lord, drawing from His living water and producing His fruit. This principle is confirmed in Jeremiah 17:7-8 as well. It speaks of the one who is willing to trust in God. Such a person will be a strong, deep-rooted plant with green leaves and everbearing fruit – living without worry or fear as they press in with confidence to the Lord.

So I bought a packet of marigold seeds. I keep it in my Bible. It's my daily reminder of the kind of seed I want to plant and the kind of plant I want to be.

"Blessed is the one who does not walk in step with the wicked... That person is like a tree planted by streams of water, which yields its fruit in season and whose leaf does not wither..." – Psalm 1:1-3

4.3

Prayer & Trust, Part 1: *A Bit About Prayer*

During graduate school in Indiana, I was given the opportunity by a missions-sending organization to volunteer with a college ministry for a year. I prayed about it and felt confident the Lord was giving me the green light to say yes. But there was a problem. I didn't have a year. I would be returning to Wyoming in six months, after finishing my Master's degree. I had set up a student teaching stint back in my hometown for the spring. No college there. How could I complete the other half of my one-year commitment?

Long story short, God opened a door allowing me to switch to a college town for my school-system internship. It so happened that I already knew the director of the local college ministry. We'd been friends back when I was doing my undergrad studies at the University of Wyoming. As soon as I knew I would be headed his way, I tried to call him. It was a Friday. No answer. Later that evening I tried again several times, but no joy. Multiple attempts on Saturday were also unsuccessful. Finally, on Sunday afternoon, I got ahold of him.

"Ken, guess what?"

"You're coming to work with me," he said matter-of-factly.

What? How could he possibly know that? I hadn't even stayed in contact with Ken for the past couple of years. "Did someone tell you already?" I asked incredulously.

"No. But this morning I was praying, asking God to bring someone here to disciple young women on campus. I just figured you were God's answer."

I was completely shocked to realize that the Lord had obviously choreographed bringing this all together so quickly. "This is incredible! I mean, doesn't it just blow you away?"

"Not really. I serve a God Who answers prayer."

Well now, that response certainly shut down my verbalized astonishment, but inwardly I was still reeling with amazement at our mysterious, incomprehensible and omnipotent God.

I share that story because it's an example of one of the great mysteries of prayer. I ask you this: When did God have the answer to Ken's prayer? On Friday, right? Two days *before* he prayed it. But remember, I wasn't able to get in touch with him until Sunday, *after* he decided to send up his petition for help. God already answered *my* prayer, by providing a place for me to complete my remaining time of ministry commitment. But this orchestrated delay contacting Ken allowed God even more praise, more glory, as He responded to this second request.

If the Lord prompts you to pray for something, it is often because He already has the answer waiting. In Mark 11:24, Jesus declares, "*...whatever you ask for in prayer, believe that you have received it, and it will be yours.*" Believe that you *have already* received it. Jesus also demonstrated the truth of this when He raised Lazarus from the dead. Before He called Lazarus to come forth, Jesus thanked His Father for what God *had already* done (Jn. 11:41-44).

I have seen this principle born out several other times in obvious ways. Once was when Dave and I were praying that the financial support for his ministry position would increase to the minimum required by our organization's governing board. The same day, we discovered that a friend had recently begun to support our ministry monthly, but we were not informed of it until *after* praying. Another time we were praying together, asking God to raise up somebody willing to speak at our large group meeting on the college campus. As we were sitting there, an acquaintance of ours called and said he'd been trying to contact us to see if we needed… you guessed it, anyone to speak to our students. When God prompts you to pray, you probably ought to – then keep your eyes peeled in anticipation of His ready, His *already,* response.

"He said, 'Daniel… you had no sooner started your prayer when the answer was given…" – Daniel 9:22-23 (MSG)

"I will answer them before they even call to Me. While they are still talking about their needs, I will go ahead and answer their prayers!" – Isaiah 65:24 (NLT)

4.4

Prayer & Trust, Part 2: *A Bit About Trust*

One of my biggest learning moments, as it pertains to prayer and trusting God, came only a few months later. In fact, I was still doing my student teaching in Casper. There was an opening for a speech/language pathologist in my school district, so I interviewed for the position. At the same time, I was applying for jobs in other places. I soon got offered a job in another town, but I was actually still hoping for the position in Casper. I liked the city and the people I worked with, and I loved volunteering for the ministry at Casper College. I then resolved to go up on the mountain just south of town and spend my Saturday praying about whether to take the current job offer, or turn it down in hopes of getting this local position.

I decided to call the man who had been a mentor to me since my early days as a college student at UW. His name was Dave. I told him my dilemma and asked his advice.

"Well, you might come down that mountain tomorrow knowing exactly what you need to do. Or maybe you won't know the correct choice yet, but instead feel a certain peace from the Holy Spirit that He will reveal it in due time. You could, however, come down the mountain after praying all day and not know any more than when you drove up there. And that's because sometimes God doesn't care."

God doesn't care? I pulled the phone away and stared at it. *Who was this man?*

"Uh, Dave?"

"Now let me tell you what I mean. Let's say you have an apple in one hand and an orange in the other, and you ask God, which one should I eat? He's probably not going to say, eat the apple. He doesn't care which one you eat because you can eat either one and still do His will."

I believe God used Dave to teach me a new lesson about prayer right then because that was exactly what was going to happen. I returned from my day of prayer not feeling any more certain about my choice than when I headed up the mountain. So I petitioned the Lord: *Okay God, I'm going off of what I just learned about prayer and I'm going to call on Monday to decline the other job offer. I want to stay here so that I can volunteer and disciple college students! I'm asking You for this job in Casper.*

It wouldn't be hard to guess what happened next. The day after I declined the out-of-town job, I was given the open position in Casper. God honored my preference and set me on a path of discipleship that has continued for many years – even beyond my retirement from the school district. From personal experience, I can tell you that as we mature as believers, there will be more and more choices where the Lord allows us to step out in faith, making wise, experienced decisions, and trusting Him to guide us along the way.

You are never going to believe it, but up until this very moment, as I finished writing these two devotionals on prayer and trust, I had never seen a connection between both events. Because I have always told each of these stories for very different reasons. Different points. Different lessons.

But wow. The full thread of God's sovereign plan is now finally clear to me. And it's embarrassingly obvious. I'm pretty certain that Ken didn't ask God to send someone to Casper College for just a few months. I sincerely doubt that he prayed for the Lord to provide simply a temporary helper. No, he wanted someone who would love discipling young women enough to stick around, to stay on for good. Well, God heeded Ken's prayer for longevity. I am still volunteering in that college ministry, a thousand years later, eagerly discipling the young women who show up at our campus each fall.

And there I was, thinking *I* was the one making big life decisions all on my own. My God is kinda sneaky sometimes.

"For I know the plans I have for you," declares the Lord, "plans to prosper you and not to harm you, plans to give you hope and a future." – Jeremiah 29:11

MAY 5.1

Prissy

When I was growing up, our closest neighbor happened to be a quirky old sheepherder named Charlie, whose property bordered ours. He was a hermit by all accounts, taking a bath only once a year in the local hot spring thermal pools and then donning a brand-new pair of overalls, which he never removed till the next bathing season. You think I'm joking.

Every once in a while, Charlie would bring us a bum lamb whose mama didn't have enough milk to share. So we'd nurse it along until it was thriving and old enough to return to the flock. One year he brought us another newborn ewe lamb, who quickly won our hearts.

We named her Priscilla, but we never called her anything except Prissy. Now she may have been a bum lamb, but I can tell you that we were never bummed about taking care of her. We put warm milk in a soda bottle every day and took turns feeding Prissy during the spring and early summer. She soon became part of the family, a favored pet, running up to us whenever she heard us call, "Here Prissy, Prissy! Here Prissy, Prissy!" She definitely acted much more like a dog than a sheep. Prissy would play in the yard with us and follow us around while we did our chores. Once school started up in the fall, she took to chasing after our big yellow school bus as we rode off each morning.

At last, it was time to return Prissy to the flock. This was certainly difficult, but just another accepted part of living in the country and we were used to it. A year or two went by, and one day my sister and I were out riding our horses in a field adjacent to Charlie's property. On the other side of the fence was a sizable flock of about 500 sheep, grazing lazily in a large pasture. I knew that Prissy was one of them. "Here Prissy, Prissy! Here Prissy, Prissy!" I called several times, just for kicks. All of those sheep just kept right on eating. After a moment though, one ewe hesitantly raised her head and kind of looked around like maybe she had something to do, some place she ought to be. I called again, but she eventually just went back to eating. The memory was too distant.

Now isn't that a pretty clear picture of what can happen to us? As long as we stay close to the Shepherd – being fed and cared for daily, given status as part of the family – we will obey Him, recognizing His voice and heeding His call. If we're not careful, however, we can slowly drift away, joining the lazy masses and ceasing to have a consistent daily time in prayer and God's Word. That great Shepherd, Who knows what is best for us, continues to call out with a voice of guidance and instruction.

Here child! Here child! Follow Me!

I really don't want to be the one who has chosen to follow the world instead, and over time created such a great distance that I no longer recognize His voice.

And just go back to grazing.

"...the sheep listen to His voice. He calls His own sheep by name and leads them out. When He has brought out all His own, He goes on ahead of them, and His sheep follow Him because they know His voice." – John 10:3-4

"My sheep listen to My voice; I know them, and they follow Me." – John 10:27

5.2

Sometimes the point of a story is not some insightful, spiritual revelation. Sometimes it's just a story. A pleasant, perhaps poignant, recollection of events such as the one below.

I was always really tight with my dad. Similar strengths and interests, same sense of humor and a mutual respect. Because of this, I often wondered if maybe my mother felt a small sense of personal neglect emanating from my general direction. A few years after I graduated from college, I wrote this short essay about my mom and gave it to her on Mother's Day. My one hope was that it might finally gift her with a much better understanding as to the central place of unique value in my life that was, and will always be, held by her only.

Snapshot of A Mother

She pauses for a moment, leans against the kitchen sink and gazes at the clock. 8:05 p.m. Once again, she's managed to miss Magnum, P.I. and there are still a million things to do before...

She sighs, and forces her tired mind to begin planning for tomorrow: lunches, money, what vehicles to take, who has what after school, and as always, what to do about dinner. As she finishes the last dish, humming to herself, a pair of teen-age arms slide around her waist and engage in a hug. A pleading and slightly guilty-sounding voice apologizes "for not helping with the dishes, Marners." Where in the world those girls had come up with that nickname for her, she'd never know. But she turns with a smile and assures her eldest daughter that no hard feelings exist about the dishes. About Magnum, maybe, but not the dishes.

From the family room comes a masculine request for a big glass of tea – *with lemon, sugar and lots of ice, please.* At the same time, from the girls' bedroom, a rather youthful voice inquires accusingly about the location of a certain pair of jeans that are desperately needed for school tomorrow. Reaching for the jar of tea, she informs her youngest child that the jeans in question are most likely in the hamper. Which, of course, leads to tears and a hurried, late-night rendezvous with the washing machine. And who gets to stay up until the laundry is done? Not to worry, she has plenty of work to do while she's waiting.

Finally, the buzz of the dryer leaves the house in rare silence – except, that is, for the continuous snoring sounds that generate from the master bedroom. On her way to join the snorer, she pauses at the door of the third bedroom. Unable to resist, she pushes the door open. Dim light spills in from the hallway to reveal twisted covers in a heap at the foot of the bed. A motionless male form lies with legs tucked under a humped back, looking vaguely like the shape of a frog. She smiles as if at some private joke, gently pulls the covers up over her sleeping son, and closes the door.

At last, she retires for the night, leaving behind a clean kitchen, clean clothes, clean dishes, and a house full of sleeping family members who are blissfully unaware that they could never make it without her.

"But we behaved gently when we were among you, like a devoted mother tenderly caring for her own children."
  – 1 Thessalonians 2:7 (AMP)

"Her children arise and call her blessed; her husband also, and he praises her."
  – Proverbs 31:28

5.3
Lessons From Brandy

The first summer after I finished grad school, I volunteered as a counselor at a church camp. It was the same camp that I had gone to every summer as a kid, and I was excited to return after all those years, as a counselor.

Over eighty campers showed up that summer. This was a week-long camp and I only got to know a few of them well. There were seven in my cabin plus a handful of others with whom I was able to build a somewhat deeper relationship – through the various small group activities and games we played, as well as afternoon free time opportunities.

Not a single kiddo in this subset of campers was named Brandy. In fact, I hadn't really connected with Brandy much at all during that week. But she must have been observing me, because on the last day, she walked up to me and asked an astonishing question: "Hey, do you know Donna Means?"

I did indeed know Donna. She was around my age, went to my church, was in my Sunday School class, and we'd become casual friends over coffee and several lunches together. My astonishment came from the fact that this young camper, Brandy, was from another state and knew absolutely nothing about me – not the city I lived in, not where I went to church, and certainly not who ate lunch with me. It turned out that my friend Donna was one of Brandy's cousins.

"Yes, I actually do know Donna! But why would you ever think to ask me that?"

"Because you act just like her." Apparently, in a thirteen-year-old's curious, complex world, this made complete sense.

Well, our conversation ended pretty quickly after that. But for several days after leaving camp, I could not stop thinking about that crazy, unexpected dialogue. For some reason, my mind just kept mulling it over, obsessing on the weirdness of it… until I finally realized there was definitely something God wanted to teach me.

In a sudden ah-ha moment I realized this: Wouldn't it be incredible if someone observing our lives just walked up to us and innocently asked, "Hey, do you know Jesus?" And it wasn't because we wore a shiny cross necklace or toted around a ten-pound Bible or had a bumper sticker boasting *John 3:16 says it all!* Instead, it was simply "because you act just like Him."

My life and actions should unmistakably remind others of Christ. People do tend to notice things. Who are they being reminded of when they watch my behavior? Or listen to what I talk about? Or observe my response to difficult situations?

Apparently, my lesson was not complete. After several more days of continuing to mentally replay my conversation from camp, the second half of God's message to me finally hit. You see, young Miss Brandy already *knew* Donna Means. Why is that important? Because no one is going to walk up to us and say, "Please tell me, *who* do you know? 'Cuz you're acting just like *someone* and I wanna know who it is."

Yes, our walk is incredibly important – but so is our talk. People need to clearly hear the gospel message as we share with them about Who Jesus is, or they will never recognize Him in our actions. Does your talk match your walk?

"And how can they hear without someone preaching to them?" – Romans 10:14b

"Whoever claims to live in Him must walk as Jesus did."
– 1 John 2:6

* Write your thoughts on the connection between walk & talk:

_____
_____
_____
_____
_____
_____
_____

5.4

Bouncing

When their grandkids were still very young, my folks would make frequent trips across the state to see my siblings and enjoy some family time with all the "littles". After one such visit, my dad shared with me a rather amusing story concerning my oldest niece, Charlie. Apparently, they were in the guest bedroom getting packed up to head back home after a weekend at my sister's house. My niece, who was around four or five years old at the time, went downstairs to where they'd been staying, so she could be entertained by watching her grandparents pack their bags. When she climbed up on the bed and began bouncing on it, my dad immediately cautioned her. "Charlie, you need to get down from there and stop jumping on the bed."

"Okay," she agreed, and kept right on jumping.

My father tried a different approach. "Sweetie, your mother has told you many times not to bounce on the bed." Crossing his arms firmly, he gave her a stern look.

"I know." Bounce, bounce, bounce.

Grandpa waited a few minutes for her to comply, but Charlie just carried on with her enthusiastic bouncing.

"Now Charlie, you know better. God does not like it when you disobey your mother."

Bounce. Bounce. Then, "Yeah, but Jesus doesn't care!"

I have to say that I laughed pretty hard when my dad told me this story. And the truth is that even at her young age, my niece was actually beginning to understand the deep meaning of grace. Granted, her application was a bit of a misuse and manipulation. But it is definitely a biblical truth that we have the profound blessing as believers to serve a grace-imparting Savior Who has already forgiven all of our sins at the cross. Having a right relationship with the Father comes not from our flawless performance or our meager attempts at perfect obedience, but solely from our position as sons and daughters. We've been grafted into His family through Christ, Who paid the ultimate price on our behalf, the required penalty of death – because only *He* had the power and authority to conquer death and bring life to those who believe.

John 14:21 makes it clear that there is an expectation of obedience for all who love the Lord. Confusion arises when we act as though obedience itself is what saves us, rather than the grace of God alone (Rom. 3:23-24). There is a second error that can also invade our thinking, namely a legalistic intrusion of supplemental rules and laws, which are nothing more than manmade regulations (Mark 7:6-8). But they clearly have no bearing on the security of our salvation.

Jesus broke the rules. Read the first few chapters of Mark and you'll see several examples. But His behaviors were not blatant acts of disobedience. His righteous actions were intentional and very effective in bringing to light the pious legalism that had long consumed the Pharisees.

Choosing obedience is certainly both biblical and important. If the one in authority says not to bounce, we ought to stop bouncing. I just think a certain five-year-old has figured out that her buddy Jesus might decide that's a silly rule, and climb up on the bed to join her.

"Whoever has My commands and obeys them, he is the one who loves Me..." – John 14:21

"Because of His great love for us, God, Who is rich in mercy, made us alive with Christ even when we were dead in transgressions—it is by grace you have been saved."
– Ephesians 2:4-5

"Isaiah was right when he prophesied about you hypocrites; as it is written: 'These people honor Me with their lips, but their hearts are far from Me. They worship Me in vain; their teachings are but rules taught by men.' You have let go of the commands of God and are holding on to human traditions."
– Mark 7:6-8

* Think through these verses concerning grace and obedience. What is your personal perspective on the biblical expectation of obedience and how it meshes with grace?

* Can you think of any verses to add?

JUNE

This month we honor our fathers. Not that they should ever be relegated to just one month. The Bible commands us to honor them all the time. At least seven verses in the New Testament speak specifically about the importance of honoring our fathers. And not just the good ones. But I was definitely blessed with a good one. It is my greatest hope and desire to honor him with my words.

Papa

*I heard someone
whistle just now.
It triggered something in my mind
and I captured a memory —
a vivid, pleasurable feeling.*

*I am just a little girl
Following in my daddy's shadow,
trying to match the rhythm of those giant footsteps
as I listen to the whistle
that echoes down the tunnels of time.*

*His big hand envelops my tiny one
Swallowing it in warm protection
with a gentle tug
that guides me along the path of my childhood.*

*And now,
quiet tears fog my vision
and I blink to try and clear my mind.
Praise God that it fails to clear away the memories.
You will always be
the number one man in my life, Papa.
I love you.*

6.1

I Love You 89

At the conclusion of the parable of the talents as recorded in the 25th chapter of Matthew's gospel, there is a powerful statement about God's gift of abundance. It is revealed in verse 29 that as believers, we will be lavished with His unfailing, overflowing richness! *"For everyone who has will be given more, and he will have an abundance..."*

There's a Cajun term called the "lagniappe" (pronounced LAN-yap), which means an extra measure; a bonus, gratuity, or unexpected benefit. The Lord has provided us with the richness of His perfect love. If we invest God's love in others, He will bestow on us the lagniappe, the extra measure. He has an endless supply of love, an abundance. There is therefore no need to hoard that love, to be stingy and hide or bury it, like the third fellow did in the parable of the talents. Likewise, it makes no sense to ever worry about what we may get as a response from the recipients of our love. Some people might choose to reject us, but God never will. We get our returned love, our abundance, from the God of the universe.

Remember the accountings in the gospels of the "loaves and fishes"? A miraculous feeding of the multitudes with a very small amount of food – which Christ's touch and blessing made sufficient on two different occasions. A very similar story can be found in the Old Testament, recorded in 2 Kings 4:42-44. In each instance, there was an incredible abundance of leftover bread and fish. It seems likely that one purpose for such a detailed narration of these particular miracles in the Scriptures is to teach us the concept of God's boundless provision. His more-than-enough.

I am firmly convinced that God is the author of the lagniappe! He *"richly blesses all who call on Him"* (Rom. 10:12). And please note that you too can imitate this principle of abundance, making practical application in your own life. Become a *lagniappe-bearer*, throwing in the unexpected and extra measure of patience, empathy and generosity when you are loving people!

My story for today comes from one of the nieces…

It started when Lizzy was just a little thing. She'd hug my brother good night and whisper, "Daddy, I love you 89!" He would look at her with a smile, give her a return hug, and tell her that he loved her also. This became quite a ritual between those two for a very long time.

But then came the day when Lizzy asked, "Daddy, are there numbers bigger than 89?"

"Yes, honey, there are. But don't worry, I know what you mean."

My brother isn't the only one who knows what it means to love someone 89. The author of the 89th Psalm reminds us that the Lord's enduring love always goes before us, standing firm and everlasting. It is incomparable, an infinite love which our heavenly Father will be faithful to maintain forever.

Even at her young age, my niece understood the message of Psalm 89. Of this I'm certain, because in response to her dad's admission about big numbers, she confidently stated, "Well then, I love you up to God."

I guess she figured there aren't any numbers bigger than God!

We lost her daddy, my brother, when Lizzy was only twenty years old. Yet sometimes I can't help but smile at the certain reassurance that *now* he has, without a doubt, a complete and perfect understanding of the lagniappe – what it truly means to be loved 89!

"I will sing of the Lord's great love forever…I will declare that Your love stands firm forever, for who… can compare with the Lord? Praise be to the Lord forever!"
– Psalm 89:1-2, 6, 52

"For I wrote to you… to let you know the abundant love that I have for you." – 2 Corinthians 2:4 (ESV)

6.2

Hope, Part 1: *When Life Is Hard*

How do you respond when life is hard? Is anxiety part of your default in tough situations?

Today's narrative does not come from my life. It originates in chapters 37-50 of Genesis and focuses on the life of Joseph, favored son of Jewish patriarch Jacob. This story has all the earmarks of a great movie: sibling rivalry, murderous plots, kidnapping, human trafficking, false accusations, and wrongful imprisonment. It then concludes in amazing fashion with dreams coming true and the good guy winning in the end. Roll credits.

When we become anxious about difficulties in life, we often make the fateful mistake of placing our hopes, desires, and worst of all, expectations, in other people and favorable outcomes. But Paul advises in I Peter 5:7, *"Cast all your anxiety on Him because He cares for you."* The Greek word for anxiety, *merimna*, can carry the same meanings as for those words just mentioned (hopes, desires, cares, worries, needs, concerns, pressures, etc.). Therefore, we are to place *all* of our anxious expectations on God *alone* because **He** cares for us.

What kinds of things make our lives difficult? Failure, job loss, financial problems, break ups, conflict, rejection, abuse, depression, loneliness, injury, cancer, death…

Let's look at our typical reactions to those trials, contrasting poor responses with right ones. Poor responses are usually reactive, band-aid approaches – medicating vices or temporary fixes such as alcohol, drugs, lashing out, bitterness, running from God, self-harm or anxiety. Right responses result from a foundational pattern of obedience and intimate relationship with God. These include time in prayer, pressing in to lean on God, embracing circumstances, seeking godly counsel, and remaining hopeful. I think a single-word description for the difference between these two types of responses is *Controlling* versus *Surrendering*.

Now let's return to the story of Joseph and take a look at what things we might learn from his responses to all the crazy difficult events in his life.

Joseph heard from God and paid attention. He always obeyed, and by persevering through early trials, attained a track record of right responses. Joseph trusted God, leaning on Him and never giving in to temptation (e.g., Potiphar's wife). He consistently showed integrity, spoke truth, recognized his inabilities and gave credit to God (Gen. 39:9-10, 40:8, 41:16). And he demonstrated compassion, forgiveness and generosity (Gen. 42:24-25, 43:16). Joseph was able to see the big picture – God's purpose in difficult times – and he was not afraid (Gen. 45:5, 50:19-21).

What *don't* we see in Joseph's responses? There was no whining, jealousy, disobedience, anger, giving up, pouting, resentment, selfishness or distancing himself from God.

Admirable. But can we replicate it? Is it possible for us to determine how Joseph was able to conquer his fears and anxiety? How he successfully eliminated all those poor responses? If you peel away the layers, it's really just one word again: Hope! Joseph abandoned *control* and instead chose *surrender.* His *hope* was in God, not in his own ability to self-manage stressful circumstances.

As difficulties and trials pierce our normal, it seems like we always want answers to the Why (…is this happening?) and the When (…will it end?). But the real answer, our best hope, is a WHO. Hope emerges as we react to hardship by looking upward to our Savior. And what is our proof that Joseph was looking upward? Well one example is clearly evidenced by his response to his brothers in the final scene of this story, which incidentally, is also the final scene in Genesis:

"You intended to harm me, but God intended it for good to accomplish what is now being done, the saving of many lives."
– Genesis 50:20

Hope, Part 2: *Riding the Surfboard*

When I first found out that my father had cancer, I made it a priority to call him every day. I didn't know how much time I had left to engage in conversations with this man. I also never anticipated how much I would be challenged as I benefitted incidentally from what God taught my father in the last eighteen months of his eighty-one years on this earth. Thus began a habit of daily, deep, theological discussions about things that matter eternally. One such dialogue began, after pleasantries, with his question of the day.

"What do you think it means to have hope?"

I thought awhile before answering. One never responded to Daddy Ray's questions with a trivial quote. After much verbal deliberation, this is what we both agreed upon. We noted that the definition of hope is very different for non-Christians, in that it is whimsical, fluctuating, and based solely on a positive outcome. In other words, getting what you want in the end. But for believers, hope is quite solid, sturdy and unmoving because it is based not on a *what* but a *Who* – not on a result, but on our faith in the Author and Ordainer of that outcome.

The same day as our dialogue on hope, Oswald Chambers' devotional *My Utmost for His Highest* had a fitting analogy. I'll paraphrase it here, along with a few of my own add-ins. If a small vessel is caught in a major ocean storm, the folks in it live in fear of huge waves that could capsize the boat. They look to the coastline, where their hope lies tethered to the distant lighthouse and a desperate need to reach the shore. A surfer, on the other hand, looks at the same storm and *rejoices* in those waves because he has another perspective. He has learned to find joy in the storm itself – not just tolerating, suffering through and hoping to survive till it's over.

True hope is like a surfboard, in that it allows us to ride life's storms minus the fear. Hope lets the believer embrace tribulation or affliction, trusting God with the outcome. If my family had adopted the secular hope I mentioned earlier, it would have died when Daddy Ray did and we would be feeling totally defeated; as our greatest desire was obviously that he would be cured. Instead, we could accept his parting and ride the waves of this tragedy because our Hope was in Christ Himself, not in getting what we wanted.

My nephew Burke once wrote a blog where he used the analogy of dropping a phone to explain the fear and anxiety that invades our thoughts when a potentially bad thing happens – like a dropped phone. Those few seconds before we pick it up to reveal if the screen is broken, are likely filled with silent begging that nothing will be damaged. His point was about broken relationships, but the notion holds true for all situations where we experience a difficult event (the drop), then become worried and fearful about the potential result (the reveal).

Hope sits quietly in the slow-motion place between the *drop* and the *reveal*. When bad things occur and I don't yet know the damage, I can place my hope in several things, but only one has merit. It is pointless to deny the drop or to beg for a favorable reveal… over which I have absolutely no influence. But I can control the space in between. If my hope is tethered to the relief of a false alarm, I will frequently face devastation. But if my hope is aligned with Who it is that makes me safe, I will find my joy in Him no matter what is revealed.

Burke ended his essay with a remark about our lives being messy and God wanting us to lay it all before Him: "The peace that occupies our hearts within the midst of our trials, comes directly from God." I'm confident his word *peace* is virtually synonymous with Daddy Ray's word *hope*. It was a good essay. Really made me think. That's what my papa always did.

Find rest, O my soul, in GOD ALONE, my Hope comes from HIM, HE ALONE is my Rock and my SALVATION; HE is my Fortress; i will not be SHAKEN. Psalm 62:5-6

6.4

Hope, Part 3: *Calming the Storm*

At the risk of being overly redundant, I want to tackle this topic one more time. And by the way, redundancy is a good thing, and certainly not scarce in Scripture. It often serves to confirm the validity or relevance of a concept, while placing extra emphasis on its importance. In Philippians 3:1, Paul states, *"it is no trouble for me to write the same things to you again, and it is a safeguard for you."*

Not long ago, my husband and I got stuck in an unexpected ground blizzard for about 40 miles on a rural Wyoming road. It is a highway we travel frequently and includes familiar hills, curves, outcroppings, and recognizable landmarks. But not on this day. We were in a total whiteout and could see nothing. The shoulder line on the edge of the asphalt was not even visible for more than about six feet ahead. If we went too fast, we might run into a vehicle traveling in front of us. Too slow, and we risked being hit from behind. It was quite unnerving and we both felt completely vulnerable.

The scariest part of all was not being able to tell how far we had come or how much longer we would be driving in this blinding snow. Without anything visual to reassure us, we felt helpless and our only hope came in crying out to Jesus.

Prayer was our lifeline to safety that day. And God was surely with us. With nowhere to look outward, we turned our fears upward and the Lord became our recognizable landmark. Hope had us fixing our eyes on Jesus (Heb. 12:2), a vertical tether rather than a lateral one.

The story narrated in Mark 4:35-41 is often entitled, "Jesus Calms the Storm." The disciples, as they cross the Sea of Galilee, become frightened by a furious squall that threatens to capsize their vessel. Fearing for their lives, they awaken Jesus, asleep on a cushion in the boat's stern, and He stills the wind and the waves with His words.

But it is His other words that fascinate me.

In all the sermons and writings and discussions I have ever been privy to concerning this passage, the point being made can be summed up by the title noted above. What miraculous authority is evidenced by The Lord of Creation as He exerts supernatural power over a violent storm! The disciples clearly knew that Jesus had the ability to save them from drowning or they never would have disrupted His sleep. But their actions also make it clear that they were placing their hope and trust in a favorable outcome – making it safely to harbor.

Please take note of Christ's words in verse 40. We can learn so much from looking at the Red Letters, and especially those where Jesus is asking questions. After calming the storm, He turns to His men.

"Why are you so afraid? Do you still have no faith?"

If life's storms make us afraid, it is because we have not realized that true faith is found in a Person, never in a promise that the tempest will cease. Real peace lies not in the absence of a storm, but in the presence of a Savior. Elisabeth Elliot once said, "The secret is Christ in me, not me in a different set of circumstances."

The truly teachable moment in this story is that Christ could have remained asleep on that cushion. He was completely at peace in the middle of a life-threatening squall. The disciples had yet to perceive that their hope, their place of safe harbor, was right there within the storm.

When we are in the midst of dark circumstances, our response must always include reaching out to Jesus. But our best hope in that moment is to realize He is already right there in the boat, holding a spot for us on the cushion.

Come sit with Me child; I AM your peace.

"Out at sea you saw God in action, saw His breathtaking ways with the ocean: With a word He called up the wind – an ocean storm, towering waves! ...Then you called out to God in your desperate condition... And you were so glad when the storm died down, and He led you safely back to harbor."
– Psalm 107:25-30 (MSG)

Notes on this past season…
* Where are you finding your hope and joy these days?
* What struggles are you dealing with?
* How is God revealing His character to you?

SUMMER

*"You have established all the boundaries of the earth; You have created **summer**…" – Psalm 74:17 (NASB)*

Summer often brings a fresh perspective. Perhaps the uncommon ability to look – as God does – at the bigger picture. Is it possible that the unexpected freedom and relaxed pace which often accompany this season will beckon us toward a greater faith? Maybe a simpler faith? Only time and experience will reveal.

A SIMPLE FAITH

I stare out the window of this old plane
at the clouds floating solemnly in blue summer sky.
      Hung carelessly,
suspended by faith in some unseen Power,
they cast dark splotches of shadow
upon the earth below.
      I long to reach out
beyond this window that separates us
and pull off a piece of fluffy whiteness,
stuff it in my bag as a souvenir.
      And later,
to press it in my scrapbook under
"Treasured Keepsakes."
Often people ask me
how I can believe in God,
in something I cannot see.
And how, since I do believe,
I see Him – what He looks like to me.
      I see God in those clouds.
I see Him in every simple, taken for granted thing.
In a mud puddle. A spiderweb. An anthill.
I see God in me, and what He's done in my life.
I hate to think what I would be now,
had He not always been there, by my side,
throughout.
      I'm not afraid to die
should this old plane just up and quit flying.
Because, like those clouds,
I have faith in something I see
not with my eyes
but with my heart.

Marvelous Marinade

Don't you just love a good marinated chicken, barbecued on the grill in the middle of summer? Well so do I! And I have to tell you that *my* marinade gets rave reviews from every guest who chomps down on that hot, juicy chicken, fresh off the grill.

Part of the secret is that my husband puts foil on the rack and crimps the edges as a cradle for the meat and sauce. It then bubbles and cooks in its juices while he carefully continues to pour any extra over the top. The meat is never dry, the aroma is always pleasing, and the flavor is delicious. Which leads to the other part of my secret, and it always begins like this:

"Wow, this chicken is so unique and incredible! Please tell me, what all do you put in your marinade?"

Dave never fails to jump in at this point with his standard response, "Whatever she can find in the kitchen!"

It's true. I have no special recipe. I just throw all of the ingredients I have available in the mix; everything that sounds yummy, like teriyaki and lime juice and Italian dressing and tamari and Worcestershire sauce and mysterious herbs and spices and on and on, till I finally get tired of adding stuff. Then I poke those chicken breasts with a fork and leave it all in the fridge to soak and absorb till it's ready, stirring every so often.

This morning while I was praying, I started to think about my identity in Christ and began praising the Lord that He IS my life – that even in the midst of turmoil, He surrounds me completely with His intimate presence, His love, His mercy. Almost immediately, a picture came to my mind.

I *am* that chunk of meat, totally submerged in a magnificent and flavorful marinade that I hope to continue soaking in, eagerly absorbing till God decides I'm ready. Christ cradles me carefully, taking the time to crimp the edges of my life –

a process that is often painful, but ensures His ongoing immersion into every part of me. The Holy Spirit may have to poke me in a few places so that more of Who He is will penetrate my soul. Then the Lord might just need to stir up some things in my life, to ensure that a greater understanding of His holiness will saturate my spirit. God certainly uses everything available to bathe His daughter in a flawless infusion of His character. And I will be given whatever length of time is necessary in order to absorb all these aspects of God's mysterious nature.

The Holy Trinity is undoubtedly the perfect mix to take my dry and tasteless soul, and stir it into something remarkable – a most beautiful, fragrant offering that will hopefully lead others to say, "Wow, your life is so unique and incredible! Please tell me what makes it so different."

"For we are to God the pleasing aroma of Christ among those who are being saved and those who are perishing."
– 2 Corinthians 2:15

"…so that by it you may grow up in your salvation, now that you have tasted that the Lord is good." – 1 Peter 2:2b-3

JULY 7.1

Norman

Some of my earliest memories as a child include packing up the family car with a picnic supper, blankets, and snacks, and heading off at dusk to the drive-in movie theater. My favorite part was getting there early enough to go hang out on the playground equipment before the movie started. My least favorite part was trying to watch a movie by peeking around the heads of whoever got to sit in the front seat.

That drive-in was still in business when I was in high school. One Friday night my brother and I, along with four of our friends, decided to go see the double feature that was playing. We drove into town, picked everyone up, and headed to the drive-in. My friend Leslie was kind enough to bring a big paper sack full of popcorn to share. After a quick trip to the concession shack for sodas, we were all ready to squish into the vehicle's darkness and watch a movie. I grabbed some of our communal popcorn and started munching away. I immediately noticed I had gotten a hair in my mouth, so I quickly got rid of it and took another bite. Felt that hair again. Or maybe it was another one. Sort of blew it out of my mouth again. When the third bite of popcorn yielded a third piece of hair, I began to notice the other occupants encountering a similar issue – lots of "phfhhh" noises, blowing, spitting, and frustrated mumbling until finally someone verbalized, "I keep getting hair in my mouth." Which was followed by a unified chorus of, "me, too!"

"Oh, wow," Leslie said. "I must have used the sack that Norman sleeps in!"

We were all very familiar with Norman. He was Leslie's huge, gray, long-haired, monstrosity of a cat. He probably weighed close to 20 pounds, and most of that was hair. I'm certain you have never seen five people pile out of a car faster than we did at that moment. Gagging, spitting, choking and coughing, wiping our mouths and hands, all of us nearly throwing up and definitely casting disgruntled glares at a sheepish-looking Leslie.

Maybe you're wondering what my purpose is in sharing this crazy story. It's just this: All of us in that vehicle were totally focused on the movie playing on the big screen, absently munching on what was supposed to be some delicious, buttery (and dare I say, hairless) popcorn. We were so engrossed in our distractions that we became quite complacent and missed the early warning signs of what turned out to be a rather significant situation.

As believers, we are each called to run the race God has marked out for us, throwing aside all things that might distract or entangle us, and diligently fixing our eyes on the goal, on the prize, on the author and perfecter of our faith, Jesus Christ (Heb. 12:1-2).

We must not be like Mary's sister Martha, who was totally preoccupied with the preparations that had to be made and thus missed out on what was most important – that of listening at the feet of Jesus (Luke 10:38-42). If we are sensitive to the prompting of the Holy Spirit, we can remain aware and involved in what's really significant. But just as in the case of Norman's sack, distractions can keep us off our guard, allowing unhealthy things to enter in, until we finally notice… after it's too late, after we've already inhaled the content.

Complacency catches us napping in places that we shouldn't!

"But Martha was distracted by all the preparations that had to be made..." – Luke 10:40

"I want you to do whatever will help you serve the Lord best, with as few distractions as possible."
– 1 Corinthians 7:35b (NLT)

"You were running a good race. Who cut in on you to keep you from obeying the truth? That kind of persuasion does not come from the One Who calls you." – Galatians 5:7-8

7.2

A Well-Edited Life

I received a clothes catalog in the mail one time, with a rather intriguingly unrelated cover photo. There were two large wooden spoons filled with what looked to be dried tea leaves. Below the picture, in an attractive, modern font, was the company's slogan: *"Ingredients of a Well-Edited Life"*

Flipping through the pages, I noticed a five foot nine-ish model, weighing maybe a hundred pounds, who was sporting some adorable sandals for $160, a lovely bead necklace (only $219) and a stylish top I'd LOVE to own, for $189 + shipping.

It got me to thinking... just exactly what are the ingredients of a well-edited life? Because I doubt that it involves reducing most of my food intake till I can fit into a stunning outfit that costs about a month's salary. I looked up the meaning of the word *edit*. The dictionary has several definitions, all related. It can mean to revise or correct, it can signify expunging or eliminating, and it can denote the adding in of something.

We have all encountered people who decided to *revise* their life choices in ways that are not very beneficial. And we certainly know folks who have opted to *eliminate* things that would have improved their lives. Some people inadvertently (or intentionally?) *add* things into their lives that will only hurt them. Might we also conclude that the mirror is a place where we've originated our own plan for a few of these poor life revisions? So how can we determine which aspects of our lives actually do require some amending?

I definitely need a life coach, or at least a handbook of some kind before I can figure out what rewrites might be necessary. Wait a minute, I already have a coach – and so do you. One definition of edit that I didn't mention earlier is "to supervise or direct the preparation of something." I have Someone who is willing to supervise the editing of how I live, to improve my function and quality, to "prepare and arrange for publication" (another definition) just exactly what the world will observe in my life. Christ Himself wants to be my life coach; to direct my heart and choices with the Spirit's influence. He uses a handbook called The Bible to *prepare and arrange* all the ingredients necessary for living that well-edited existence. Here is a list of the daily spiritual disciplines I have found to be helpful…

• Press in to the Holy Spirit as He guides • Pray Scriptural truths over yourself • Meditate on verses and passages relevant to your current situation • Listen to God speak in your prayer time • Set measurable goals and pray for them • Seek counsel for mentoring and accountability • Memorize Bible verses • Find someone to disciple • Share the gospel and your own spiritual journey with a non-believer in your life • Seek out opportunities to practice transparency, humility, vulnerability.

Not saying I do all these perfectly or consistently, but when I do, there's a noticeable difference in how well I embrace growth in my life. More importantly, it is vital to understand that it's never about *us* doing the editing. Our job is to simply remain present in the life God has already given us and then let the Master Editor provide the perfect ingredients. He may just have a revised ending to our story.

"But when He, the Spirit of Truth, comes, He will guide you into all the truth." – John 16:13a

"All Scripture is …useful for teaching, rebuking, correcting and training in righteousness, so that the servant of God may be thoroughly equipped for every good work." – 2 Tim. 3:16-17

7.3 ॐ ॐ

Galatians 2:20

Henry Blackaby was our main speaker at fall retreat that year. There was no way I was going to miss it. As you might imagine, with a famous author as the draw factor, we had the largest attendance ever at this yearly event for regional college students. I was particularly excited to see what God might say to *me* that weekend. But I'm getting ahead of myself.

It had been a really hard year. Mom's irreversible journey into Alzheimer's disease was well on its unpleasant way. And my responsibilities as primary care-giver had increased dramatically. The week prior to fall retreat was exceedingly stressful. That Monday, on the way home from another difficult evening with my mom, I called my husband in tears. Life was chaotic, to say the least. I worked full-time, worked out at the gym most days, helped my mom every evening, volunteered with our college ministry, discipled several women, and hosted a weekly small-group Bible study through our church. Way too busy. Sobbing uncontrollably on the phone, I told my husband, "I don't know how to live my life!"

That night at community group, during our time of prayer, I shared with this gathering of concerned and caring friends about my ridiculous schedule and stressors, reiterating the earlier statement I'd made to Dave, "I don't know how to live my life." And then again, a couple of nights later, I once more repeated my new mantra to all of my discipleship girls as we were sharing prayer requests. Eventually, Friday made its appearance and I left for retreat.

While Blackaby was speaking in the evening session, he referenced Galatians 2:20 and then quoted it. Only he quoted a different verse. I probably wouldn't have done much more than a head nod if he hadn't misquoted, but the discrepancy made me sit up and pay more attention. This was a verse I'd memorized years before. I thought to myself, *wait a minute, that's not Galatians 2:20. Now, how does that verse go? Oh* yeah, *"I have been crucified with Christ and I no longer live, but Christ lives in me…" yes, that's it.* And I didn't think much more about it.

In the next morning's session Blackaby again referenced the Galatians verse, but this time he actually did quote it: *"I have been crucified with Christ…"* This also caught my attention more than it probably would have, simply because of the wrong reference the night before.

About an hour later, someone else got up to speak and began sharing a story. As he was talking, his words included the phrase, "…and if you live your life…" The similarity of this phrase to my week-long mantra, caused me to repeat that recent lament in my head: "I don't know how to live my life."

Immediately, also in my head, I heard an answering voice: *"Yes, but I DO!"* followed by the words, *"I have been crucified with Christ and I no longer live, but Christ lives in me…"* I sat there in stunned silence, tears streaming down my face as I absorbed the Holy Spirit's intimate and obvious admonition. It wasn't about *my* ability to handle the chaos of my life. It was about surrendering that life to allow Christ – Who lives in me! – to do His work.

I have neglected to convey that back on Monday evening, part of our small group discussion included the question of how each of us experiences the greatest intimacy with God. I had shared with them that I feel God's intimate presence most fully whenever He takes the time to rebuke me.

Now, here He was, doing exactly that. Incredible. The God of the entire universe choosing to specifically and personally correct my thinking. I turned to Dave sitting next to me and whispered, "I can go home now. I got what I came for."

"I have been crucified with Christ and I no longer live, but Christ lives in me. The life I now live… I live by faith in the Son of God, Who loved me and gave Himself for me." – Gal. 2:20

"And if the Spirit of Him Who raised Jesus from the dead is living in you, He…will also give life to your mortal bodies because of His Spirit Who lives in you." – Romans 8:11

7.4

What You Don't Need

I went to church camp each summer as a kid. Loved it. Looked forward to it every year and made some good friends there. It was a great place to learn more about Jesus, see God's beauty in nature, build friendships, and realize the importance of having a daily devotional time, among other things. One of my most favorite *among other things* was sitting around the campfire each night, sharing stories and singing songs. I loved camp so much, in fact, that I continued my involvement as an adult, becoming a counselor several years and volunteering as camp director on a couple of occasions.

My other most favorite thing was skit night. So much fun. Laughing together, teasing each other, getting serious, being silly. And sometimes, I must admit, we liked to play pranks on the unsuspecting. There was one pranking game that always seemed to make its appearance every year – as long as there was another church camp newbie eager to be fooled. The counselors would ask for a volunteer, some gullible soul, to come up front and sit in a chair. A large sheet or blanket was draped over top to cover them completely, and then the instructions were given: "Okay, now take off something you don't need." After a bit of hesitation, out from under the blanket would come something like a shoe or a sandal. The counselor would say it again: "Now take off something you don't need." More hesitation, then maybe a sock. Again, the instruction was repeated. And again. And again. Eventually placing stronger and stronger emphasis on the words *don't need*.

Every year, it seemed, those naïve campers were willing to give up some pretty important items. Not only shoes and socks, but also hairbands, overshirts, pocket change, hoodies, glasses, watches, belts, jewelry…

It truly was pretty funny, but also, pretty pitiful. The participants didn't realize that they were completely blind to what they really ought to get rid of. Which was the blanket, of course. The leaders often had to stop the game before the poor kiddo took off so many clothes that they would end up naked and ashamed.

In Revelation 3:17-18, we hear of the shamefully naked Laodiceans, who thought they were rich and didn't need anything. *"You say, 'I am rich; I have acquired wealth and do not need a thing.' But you do not realize that you are wretched, pitiful, poor, blind and naked. I counsel you to buy from Me gold refined in the fire, so you can become rich; and white clothes to wear, so you can cover your shameful nakedness; and salve to put on your eyes, so you can see."*

God says HE is the One who can give us everything we need. Without the Lord's generous, eternally crucial supply, we are definitely shameful and needy. And like the poor, deceived camper, we can become blinded to the one thing we *do not* need – that blanket. That comfy, self-protective, manmade covering of earthly riches. There is a lesson here in the cautionary tale of the Laodiceans, who were so focused on their manufactured wealth, they were willing to "take off" the very things they *did* need – those heavenly provisions necessary for a godly life.

"...God has been gracious to me and I have all I need..."
– Genesis 33:11

* Here are a couple more verses on this topic. Write down your take on the idea of having "all that we need." Or journal about a story from your own life that reflects this concept.

"His divine power has given us everything we need for a godly life..." – 2 Peter 1:3

"God is able to bless you abundantly, so that ...having all that you need, you will abound in every good work." – 2 Cor. 9:8

_____
_____
_____
_____
_____
_____
_____
_____
_____
_____
_____
_____
_____
_____
_____
_____
_____
_____
_____
_____

AUGUST

June brides. July celebrations. August weddings. 'Tis the season for nuptials. And when we get to observe that couple's first dance, we smile at the thought of their exciting future together. Scripture has labeled God's children as the 'bride' of Christ. Think of the moment when you began your intimate relationship with Jesus. What joy to glide across that floor for the first time, twirling to the music of angels, in the loving arms of your Creator. How scuffed up are your dancing shoes these days?

First Dance

She walks into the room,
beautiful.
Not because she thinks so,
but only because someone watching
recognizes the beauty inside
enhancing the outside.
He dances with her in his mind,
across the crowded room
as she holds her head high,
laughing.
They feel the need to touch, to be one;
and he notes
that the perfection of the moment
belongs not to their love for each other,
but to a common love
for their Master,
Creator.
Will man ever experience what God intends?
Does he nurture the God-seed of love
planted in his soul?
Can he rise above the human restraints
of power and greed, of self and control;
to find the one true Love
that gives and feeds
and humbles and fulfills?
She reaches for him
in the world's vast darkness,
and nods.

8.1

Here We Go a Waddling

Did you know that a group of ducks is called a waddling? Actually, there are many group names for ducks. I just like the term *waddling* the best. But it's a label only given to ducks when they're on land. When they are in water, they're called a *raft* or a *paddling*. Unique, wouldn't you say? And ducks in flight can have many other titles as well. Unexpected, right? Almost as unique and unexpected as my story for today.

"Get your shoes on. Grab some bread. C'mon now, hurry up and get in the truck!"

My father had just rushed back to the house from way out in the pasture where he'd been irrigating that afternoon. He wouldn't say why. So we simply obeyed. All three of us kids jumped in the back of our old beater pick-up and off we raced up the hill, around the corner, across the cattle guard, down the bumpy dirt road, hanging on for dear life to the sides of the truck bed and our bag of bread.

We finally reached the irrigation ditch, stopping near the place where my father was working. His tarp had dammed up some dirty canal water, and there in the unintentional wading pool was a mama duck with about twelve itty bitty ducklings. Slowly, quietly, carefully, we crept close enough to toss some torn off pieces of bread into the water. At first, Mama Mallard swam away in fear, but eventually came back to investigate. Pretty soon, her brood joined her at the newly christened 'feeding trough'. We watched in utter amazement and joy as those little tykes gobbled up all of our bread. What a treasure, a unique and unexpected blessing to watch this *raft* of little ones as they paddled around chasing chunks of white.

We went back every day, of course, armed with more groceries. Usually bread, but sometimes popcorn or other ducky edibles – we were bonding as a family as we all watched and fed this other family, and building a much-treasured memory together. After a week or so, the ducklings were no longer afraid of us. Several more days and the whole waddling would immediately head toward us as soon as they saw the pick-up coming. It wasn't long before our web-footed friends, who weren't so itty bitty anymore, started chasing that truck down the road. It was almost comical.

Then came the day we only counted ten or eleven. Next day, only about eight showed up for dinner. Soon it was four or five and then none. Just like that, they were all gone. Sad for us, but not for them. Those twelve ducklings discovered their wings. The waddling had left the ground to embrace their vagabond life as a skein in the skies. Yes, a *skein*. Look it up.

Now that's a heart-warming story, to be sure. But are there lessons to be learned? I believe so. I remember the first time I was prodded and cajoled into leading a Bible study, followed by a firm, convincing request to disciple college students. It was a unique opportunity, definitely unexpected, and a long, bumpy road till I ever felt confident that God might use me to feed those girls what they needed in order to grow spiritually.

But it is always the Lord Himself who supplies the Bread of Life. We are just the blessed ones who get to toss it out for our eager learners to gobble up. They might begin with a little fear and trepidation about what is coming their way. Yet once they taste the yumminess of Scripture, as the Holy Spirit reveals the deep Truths of the faith, our little "ducklings" will chase after more of it. Such discipling relationships often have the benefit of building a family together and creating treasured memories.

If you are the one mentoring, you will eventually have the pleasure of watching your brood try out their wings. It can be hard to let go, when you know you're no longer needed. Sad for the mentor. But not for them. They are now ready to fly, to lead others, to discover and embrace God's call on their life.

Yet I am confident, that by the grace of God, there will be more waddlings in your future.

"...as a nursing mother cares for her children, so we cared for you. Because we loved you so much, we were delighted to share with you not only the gospel of God but our lives as well." – 1 Thessalonians 2:7-8

8.2

Identity, Part 1: *Good, Good Father*

Everyone knew him. He was the high school math and science teacher, he was a preacher, flight instructor and rancher, he was very involved in his church and eventually, he was in the state legislature. He was my father.

Everybody – and I mean everybody – knew my dad. When I got introduced to folks, it was always just "This is Ray Harrison's daughter." I started giving him a hard time about it because I thought it was unfair that I didn't get my own name, I was just the daughter. I even had a high school chemistry teacher who never called me anything except Ray's Baby. Seriously. When he called on me in class, he'd say, "Hey, Ray's Baby, what do you think?" I'm not even sure he knew my real name. (kidding about that last part.)

After college, I got my first job and moved away from my hometown. A man I was acquainted with from my new church had to go to Cheyenne during a session of state legislature. He introduced himself to my dad and then said, "You're Janelle's father, right?" My dad started laughing out loud and called me on the phone right away. "You're never going to believe it! You finally got called by your *actual name* and I was the one being called *your father*!" We both chuckled a lot about that.

A few years ago, I was at one of our college ministry's fall retreats. Arriving rather late, I had to sneak in the back. I sat next to a director from another campus. He leaned over and quietly introduced me to a new couple who were considering coming on staff. He told them, "This is Dave's wife." Well, of course all those memories came flooding back and I jokingly argued, "Oh no, I'm not *his wife*. He's *my husband!*" We all just laughed and then went to singing right away, since the session was starting. The first song we sang was one I had not at that point ever heard before. The chorus says, *He's a Good, Good Father – that's Who He is.* But there's another line that ends with *that's who I am, that's who I am, that's who I am.* The minute I heard those words, I just wanted to roll my eyes. I don't like worship songs focused on my needs, on me, me, me, and very little on God Himself. I was certainly ready to not like this song, but the Holy Spirit suddenly stopped me: *you need to pay attention to these words.* I realized we were singing about a fundamental truth that God is good, and that He's our *Father*. That's Who He *IS*. The next words were simply noting that I'm loved by Him. *That's* who I am. All you need to know about me is summed up in this declaration. *I'm loved by God!* Personally. Intimately. If someone ever comes up to me and asks, "Who are you?" I can say to them, "Well, all you really need to know about me is I'm loved by a holy God – that's who I am." And He's a good, good Father, perfect in all His ways. My identity is a daughter who belongs to the God of the universe. Now that's just crazy cool.

And I belong to my dad. I am Ray's Baby. What an honor! There's nobody else who can say that. Likewise, I'm Dave's Wife. Wow! Not one other person gets that privilege or pleasure. It's just so amazing to think of it that way. How incredibly special it is to be known as belonging to, and being loved by God Himself – by Jesus. That's where I get my identity. That's who. i. am.

"We know, dear brothers and sisters, that God loves you and has chosen you to be His own people."
 – 1 Thessalonians 1:4 (NLT)

"And you belong to Christ; and Christ belongs to God."
 – 1 Corinthians 3:23 (NASB)

8.3

Identity, Part 2: *Pitching Your Tent*

Who do you belong to? Where are you finding your identity? Can you please settle in to the realization that you, yes you, bear God's name? You are His! His *child*. What if you could just camp out right there, pitching your tent in the lap of God and reveling in your identity as a son or daughter of the Father?

Instead, most humans yearn to step out of that tent. We wander off into the woods, trying to "find ourselves." We start roaming down different trails, desperately looking for the right path. What becomes clear, after drilling down a bit, is that we're all simply trying to feel in control. However, those enticing woods soon become awkward and uncomfortable and, quite frankly, a bit scary. Why? Because we don't belong there. Yet these very same paths can easily become idols for us, where we endeavor to find our own identity.

When I was young, we had an Australian Blue Heeler named Kip. We took him camping for the first time when he was just a puppy. My family always preferred a dispersed-style of camping, deep in the mountains in the middle of some forested nowhere. The minute we started setting up our campsite, Kip jumped out of the truck and took off barking. He was on a quest to become one brave, adventurous, tough guy and go battle the world on his own. Only, all the critters out in those woods were quite a bit bigger and tougher than he was. Within minutes young Kippy came racing back to camp and positioned himself under the truck, ferociously barking and growling from his place of safety.

Now why aren't we smart enough to do that? To return to our place of safety – the lap of God – where our true identity is found. Instead, we keep venturing out on wrong roads, and then when we can't determine what is amiss, we begin experiencing undiagnosed feelings of discouragement and anxiety. The wrong-road sequence happens like this: We vacate the sheltering lap of our good, good Father and start out on a misguided quest for identity, a foolish and unfortunate attempt to find our worth and value in created things rather than the Creator. That erroneous place of belonging leads to fear, chaos and anxiety, and at some point, anxiety itself becomes our idol. So instead of realizing our identity in Christ, we start finding our identity in Crisis!

Where do we go searching for this identity? Maybe in our friends, family, career, appearance, skills, success... I'm sure you could list plenty more. When one of these becomes an idol, steering the focus of where we're headed in life, it will likely result in failure and an identity crisis. In John 14:6, Jesus states, *"I am the Way, the Truth, and the Life."* He says *"I am"* six different times in that chapter. Thomas and Philip seem a bit worried, perhaps discouraged, at this point in their journey with Christ. They anxiously ask Him *where* He is going. *"How can we know the way to go?"* And what does Jesus tell them? *I am the where, I AM the WAY.*

I do believe that not all identity-crisis anxiety is bad. Sometimes, it is the Holy Spirit intentionally creating in us an uncomfortable inner realization that we don't belong here – wherever here is, the path we've chosen. Deuteronomy 28:65 says, *"you will find no repose, no resting place for the sole of your foot. There the Lord will give you an anxious mind..."* Unrest can actually lead us straight back to the lap of God!

Jeremiah 17:8 says a tree rooted by the stream doesn't worry about heat or drought, and never fails to bear fruit. We need not be anxious about work, success, relationships, the future, our appearance, etc. if we plant our roots – if we pitch our tent in that safe Protector's campsite where we belong.

"Whoever wanders from the path of understanding will end up where the dead are gathered." – Proverbs 21:16 (ISV)

"...God the Father...loves you and keeps you safe in the care of Jesus Christ." – Jude 1:1 (NLT)

"...live with us in the Lord's own land, where His sacred tent is located..." – Joshua 22:19 (CEV)

8.4

It Is Well

I wrote an essay several years ago entitled "It Is Well." It was a detailed account of some events that happened a short while before and after the death of my mother. We had been forced to make the difficult choice of placing her in a nursing home for better care and monitoring. God did miraculous things during that time, continually reassuring us that in spite of all our difficulties in life, He always makes it well in our souls. I've included a short excerpt here:

I cried a lot that first night, having left my mom alone in a strange place where her worldly possessions were reduced to a chair, a pillow and a small blanket. The next day, my sister and I were in a store and I saw a beautiful plaque on which was painted, "It is well with my soul." It was turquoise – mom's favorite color. I thought, it may not be so otherwise, but it certainly is well with her soul. I purchased it to hang over her bed in this new place, which was disappointingly similar in size and appearance to a shared hospital room. On Sunday I hung the plaque, comforted by the symbolism that God was indeed watching over her. The next day, my sister-in-law texted to see how mom was doing. I shared about the plaque and she replied: "You won't believe it! We sang that hymn in church yesterday. I had the thought that although not so with your mom's mind, it IS well with her soul." Almost identical to my own reflections! I replied that it must be God's sentiment as well, to give us the same exact responses. We were both quite affected by this clear message and the unique irony that I had been hanging – while Kathleen was singing – those comforting lyrics from Horatio Spafford's hymn. And soon, we would realize that the Lord had also been preparing our own souls with His comfort.

One day, my husband's folks were in town. I handed the essay to my mother-in-law, eager for her to be encouraged by this incredible story. Instead, she scanned the pages quickly. My father-in-law entered the room and urged her to hurry up.

"You need to get going – we have a lot of stuff to do."

While he chatted with his son, my distracted reader chimed in occasionally on their unrelated topic, casually glancing at the pages and flipping through them hurriedly as she continued to listen to their discussion. She soon set the story aside and headed off to her tasks for the day. I was totally disheartened to see her rush through and treat so lightly the words I had penned, which came from my heart during an emotionally painful time. I excused myself and went to another room, trying hard not to cry. Opening my Bible, I asked the Lord to forgive my pouting heart. He indeed forgave and then He taught. As I read His Word, my hurt began to dissolve and I was soon ready to listen…

Years ago, the Lord wrote an extensive essay, a personal and detailed compilation of 66 books, which He has given to us to read. He gets excited whenever we pick it up, hoping we will take the time to settle in and be encouraged by His incredible Story. When we scan the pages quickly, in a hurry to "get going because we have a lot of stuff to do", it saddens Him. Distracted by things around us, we enter the world's conversations, and fail to concentrate on the discourse of Scripture. How disheartened He must be when we treat lightly those words penned deep from the heart of our Lord.

Father, help me stay present and attentive in Your amazing story, woven for us through Scripture. May I never be pulled into a shallow, fleeting perusal of Your life-giving Word. Amen.

"Your Words were found and …became for me a joy and the delight of my heart; for I have been called by Your name, O Lord God of hosts." – Jeremiah 15:16 (NASB)

SEPTEMBER 9.1

Solid Food

I love memorizing Bible verses. I know hiding God's Word in my heart is very important, confirmed scripturally, and immensely helpful in shaping me to be more like Jesus. I used to be really consistent at memorizing and then reviewing my verses every single day. Not so daily anymore, as I seem to be stricken with a bad case of OBS... Old Brain Syndrome. But back in the day, I was learning about 2-3 new verses per week. I would faithfully review them in my car wherever I went.

One morning, I was driving somewhere and working on my verses. A few days earlier I'd gotten in a conversation with my roommate Amy, on the topic of mentoring. Her boss at Youth For Christ had told her that every believer should have a more mature Christian pouring into their life. I was discipling Amy, but who was mentoring me? At that time, I didn't know of anyone I could ask and suddenly it had me worried. I was in a weekly small group Bible study, listening to sermons every Sunday, consistently committed to my daily time with God in prayer and personal Bible study, but was that enough?

Now here I was, half-distracted, tooling down the highway, glancing at references on my verse cards and then trying to say them from memory. Hebrews 5:14 was my next card. I quoted it to myself: "But solid food is for the mature, who by constant use, have been trained to distinguish good from evil." Then several quick peeks to see if I had said it correctly.

But solid food... yep. *Is for the mature...* check. *Who by constant use...* got it. *Have trained themselves...* oh yikes, quoted that part wrong. It's not "been trained", it's *trained themselves* – wait, say that again? It's not "been trained", it's *trained themselves.* Let me think about that – they haven't <u>been</u> trained by another, they've trained <u>themselves</u>. Hmmm. Solid food is for *mature* believers, who've *trained themselves* to know and do good, never evil (by constant use, gaining wisdom through the solid food of God's Word and prayer).

Lightbulb moment. God was showing me I didn't have to panic about my current mentor-less situation. That there may be times in life when we are unable to find someone older and wiser who is willing to take the time to pour into us. But God is never limited by circumstances. Through the Holy Spirit, He can teach us directly from Scripture and our time in prayer. My second lightbulb moment came as I realized that the Lord was doing this very thing right then! He was using His solid food (my current memory verse) and my goofed-up misquote to teach me this very concept.

Since learning this, there have been several stretches of time when I have been without a mentor. But God has also blessed me through the years with people who have willingly poured into me, challenging me to grow spiritually. I am especially thankful for Carolyn, the lady who mentored me faithfully over the last ten years or so. I'm equally thankful God has called me to disciple those younger women He puts in my path. I hope to guide them toward a maturity where they realize they can *train themselves* to distinguish good from evil, to reject the wrong and choose what is right (Isaiah 7:15).

"We do, however, speak a message of wisdom among the mature... God's wisdom, a mystery that has been hidden... revealed to us by His Spirit. The Spirit searches all things, even the deep things of God." – 1 Corinthians 2:6-7, 10

9.2

A Jeep and a Blind Man

She came into this world quite suddenly, and several weeks ahead of schedule. Barbara Rose. A beautiful name for a beautiful baby girl. It scared us though. She was just a tiny thing, stuck in a really big hospital with some really big tubes stuck in her. My brother's first child and she was a miracle.

My favorite Barbie story happened when she was about four years old. My husband and I went to visit her family in Colorado over Easter. Barbie came running out to greet me, and as I lifted her into my arms, she exclaimed, "Dess what? We dot a deep!" Now I already knew they got a jeep, but I acted surprised. "Where is it? Can you show it to me?"

"It's in the darage!" So off we went to the garage – which was actually a large shop behind their house – in search of this new vehicle. When we stepped inside the garage, however, there was no jeep. I said, "Oh no, it's missing." To which my niece replied, "Yeah, somebody musta stode it!" Then she looked at me with big eyes and proclaimed, "It's a *mystery*!"

Well, turns out nobody stole the jeep, but it sure gave me a tickle to have this dialogue with the little one. And there are a few lessons here for all of us. Such as, how quickly we jump to wrong conclusions when things aren't as we expect. I mean, it's one thing for a small child to assume the worst, but why do we still as adults immediately want to accuse, to avoid any investigating before we point the finger? If someone treats me poorly or responds in an unpleasant, insulting way, I can be instantly offended or I can take the time to consider what may be causing their reaction; what things are going on "behind the scenes" in their life. Or what if it's really on me, and I'm simply misreading their tone or their words? Just a thought.

Lesson number two: When facing unexpected, disagreeable situations, approach them as my niece did. She didn't stay mired in the negative blame-it-on-a-burglar phase for long. A mentor once told me to "eat the mystery." I think Barbie already had that part figured out. She wanted to investigate, explore and discover. Maybe I should learn to see my messy, bewildering and potentially scary life-changes as opportunities to engage the mystery, to follow God as He leads me on unforeseen adventures. The wild ride might just be worth it.

My other Barbie story happened much more recently. She's now in her mid-twenties. Lives in the same city as her favorite aunt, so I have lots of opportunities for dialogues and lessons learned. One day, Barbie was excited to tell me about having just read the Bible story recorded in John 9:1-11, where Jesus puts mud on a man's eyes to heal him. There are actually several instances in the New Testament where people have their vision restored by Christ, by His words, His touch, even His saliva. But in this particular biblical event, Jesus used something apart from Himself. He used mud.

As she was studying this passage, the Lord did a nifty little mic drop into my niece's mind and heart. What do we know about mud? It's dirty. Ordinary. It is tromped on, ugly, unclean and undesirable. We also know that mud originates from dust of the earth – as did mankind. And what did our Lord choose as an instrument to bring sight to this man? The ugly and undesirable. The ordinary.

God uses imperfect humans – His chosen – to bring sight to those who are spiritually blind. He made us His instruments of healing and wholeness, and He has clearly used my ordinary niece to open *my eyes* in understanding. Color me thankful.

"Don't let anyone look down on you because you are young, but set an example for the believers in speech, in life, in love, in faith and in purity." – 1 Timothy 4:12

"...they saw the courage of Peter and John and realized that they were unschooled, ordinary men..." – Acts 4:13

Grandmother

That's what she preferred to be called. Born in 1902, she survived two world wars, the Great Depression, and a poverty that defined turn-of-the-century farm life. She loved to climb and explore, and as a teen, hiked up the highest peak in the Big Horn Mountains with all of her sisters.

By age seventeen, she had begun teaching in a one-room schoolhouse in rural western Nebraska. She married young, soon had two children, and moved to Texas where her husband ran off with a "tavern lady" when my mom was in the second grade. She got a secretarial job and raised her children alone on homemade meals, handsewn clothes and solid Christian principles.

When I was quite young, my grandmother retired from her life in Dallas and moved up near us in Wyoming. She showed me how to grow plants, crochet, read my Bible and pray. She taught me to sew, cook, can vegetables, and most importantly, to get my nose out of that book and appreciate the beauty of God's creation! Whenever any of us grandkids made a mistake or messed something up, she'd shrug it off and say, "You'll never notice it on a galloping horse!"

Grandmother was prim, stoic, disciplined, and never still. She liked hummingbirds, summer in the mountains, wild roses, and the color blue. Sundays meant flowered dresses, hats with matching shoes, and a proper trip to church – God's house.

Grandmother loved her family and she loved the Lord. Those who knew her well might use words like *unselfish, determined, honest, humble, never wasteful*. She was a gifted seamstress and a hard worker who hated to inconvenience anyone. She grew her own vegetables, mowed her own lawn, and stubbornly walked to the grocery store because it was "only a couple of miles and Lord knows you don't need to drive there – that's what He gave you two good feet for!"

When I was in high school, I would visit her during my lunch hour once a week for leftovers that never tasted like leftovers. Grandmother's home was always clean and tidy, with a pleasant aroma of lavender and oatmeal cookies.

One day as I entered, I heard her on the phone having a very civilized disagreement with what turned out to be my mother. It apparently didn't end in much of a truce, because when she hung up the phone, she looked at me, shook her head and stated wistfully, "Your mother just doesn't listen to me anymore." That was my grandmother's subtle sense of humor.

It started with simple forgetfulness, repeated questions and household chores left undone. We watched helplessly as death slowly took her mind six years before it stole her body. At the end, my weekly visits were to my ailing grandmother's new one-room home – no more leftovers, but I faithfully brought her ice cream that I fed to her with a spoon. I looked into those vacant eyes and talked about everything and nothing. I smiled at her, told her I loved her and reminded her that I was her granddaughter. I held her hand and kissed her on the forehead and always promised to return soon.

Less than a month before her eighty-ninth birthday, it was Jesus holding her hand as she made one last proper trip to God's house. I believe in the prosperity gospel because of my grandmother – I just think most people have a terrible misunderstanding about what it is that makes us prosperous. She taught me to notice the riches of Scripture, to appreciate the opulence of God's scenic creation, to enjoy the prosperity of family, and to value the affluence of giving more than you take. My life is all the richer for having known her.

"Even when I am old and gray, do not forsake me, my God, till I declare Your power to the next generation, Your might to all who are to come." – Psalm 71:18

"Gray hair is a crown of splendor; it is attained by a righteous life." – Proverbs 16:31

* Please take a moment here to write about your own grandmother. Or maybe it's a grandfather. Aunt, uncle, family friend... someone you admired, learned from, looked up to when you were young. Your hero. Record some of your best memories. Express how and why this person had such an impact on your life.

    Maybe you even have more than one? Write about both…

_____
_____
_____
_____
_____
_____
_____
_____
_____

(more space on the next page)

* Are you carrying on the legacy of those who have gone before you?

Let me go all CSI on you for a minute. Where have you scattered your footprints? Where have you left your DNA? What have you touched that will reveal your True identity to those investigating your life? We all leave a legacy. When you depart this earth, what will witnesses testify about you? What will the jury study and learn?

Here's another way to process it: Make a list of the qualities you possess that others might look up to and learn from. Are there any additional traits you want to cultivate?

> Warning: This story is a little longer and it is about cats. You may not love them, but God sure does.

Cats, Cats, and More Cats

"When a man loves cats, I am his friend and comrade, without further introduction." – Mark Twain

It was a wonderful thing to grow up on a ranch. I learned how to live well, love much and laugh long. I learned how to lean on my family through all the ups and downs of country life. God blessed us with so many of His creatures. We had cattle, horses, a donkey named Poco, baby lambs in the spring, chickens and sheep and dogs and cats. Plenty of cats. In fact, there was a time when we had fourteen at once.

My sister had a gray cat called Ginger. I named my calico Snoopy. They both ended up pregnant and had six kittens apiece on the very same day. We quickly made beds out of cardboard boxes carpeted with rags, and separated the two moms and their babies. But every time we went to check on them, they had moved all twelve kittens back into one box. After several attempts to split up this feline commune, we reluctantly abandoned the second box. Snoopy and Ginger both had a plan and a system. One of them would lay in the box and feed all the kittens, while the other would head off to chase mice or explore fields or do whatever it is that cats do when they know we're not watching. Sooner or later, that mama would return. As soon as she stepped into the box, the other would step out, off to see the world and take a break from minding babies. Only God could create animals with such ingenuity and teamwork.

A few years later, someone gave us a stray cat they had found on their doorstep. He didn't arrive with a name, so we christened him Matthew. His hair was long and mostly black, interrupted by occasional spikes of white. We all fell instantly in love with that cat. Matthew had a very trusting nature and he knew without a doubt we would always take care of him. He loved to be held and stroked, and he definitely loved to purr.

He also loved to eat. All of our cats were outdoor pets, but sometimes mom would let us bring them inside to eat their food – if it was really cold out and we begged hard enough. I've never seen a cat eat more or faster than Matthew. He would gobble down every precious bite as quickly as possible, until he had an underbelly approximately the size of a small cantaloupe. Then he would slink quite shamefully into our living room and hide behind the piano until his tummy size was less embarrassing. Oh, how that cat made me smile.

We adopted another homeless kitty not too long after that. By this time, my brother was in his first semester of college. One weekend he came home for a visit, but he wasn't alone. A cat had been hanging around the dorms that fall and my brother decided it needed a better home. Interestingly, this cat looked very similar to our previous stray, with long, black hair and streaks of white in odd places. He jumped right out of my brother's Jeep and immediately scrambled up on top of our house somehow. That crazy kitty earned himself a new name by deciding he was going to live on our roof. Fiddler had found his forever home.

At first, Fiddler was quite shy and skittish, but he soon became part of the family. He was playful and friendly and, just like his predecessor, always ready to purr. Besides the roof, Fiddler loved climbing on the backs of our horses to stay warm in the winter. He also loved to hang out in the garden. He especially enjoyed the cucumbers, that strange cat of ours, so we were forced to keep him quarantined every fall.

And he loved leaves. My sister and I discovered a great Fiddler game, quite by accident. It started with an overdue leaf-raking chore and ended with a mischievous cat pouncing on our newly formed piles. The game's rules went something like this:

First, my sister and I get down on our knees, using our hands to rake up a big pile of leaves. Fiddler watches and waits from a safe distance of maybe 20 feet away, snapping his tail in anticipation. When the pile is big enough, we both slap our hands on the ground and shout, "C'mon!" Fiddler chases toward us and leaps head first into the leaves. We all wrestle and fight and tussle and tickle until the pile is no longer a pile. Then Fiddler shakes himself off, retreats to his perch and we start all over again. The game always ends when the cat gets bored and simply abandons his minions.

Yes, it was a wonderful thing to grow up on a ranch. God surely blessed us in many ways, shielding us from accidents and serious injury and rattlesnakes and poverty and monotony and loneliness. He taught us to love family, protect animals, trust others, be playful, take risks, shelter the homeless, and to heed the unfortunate consequences of eating too much.

"God made all sorts of wild animals, livestock, and small animals... And God saw that it was good."
– Genesis 1:25 (NLT)

AUTUMN

*"...rejoice in the LORD your God, for He has given you the **autumn** rains because He is faithful." – Joel 2:23*

Fall is here. Oh my. Exquisite and stunning evidence of this has spread itself all around us in nature. The phrase "swan song" comes to mind. According to ancient folklore, swans will sing most beautifully right before they die. It is likewise obvious that God's artistic yearly creation embraces the idea of leaving autumn behind in style. Are you becoming more brilliant and beautiful as your seasons of life advance?

The Way of Things

Summer has ghosted me.
Again.
It's firmly fall and my bright red maple
reluctantly begins its annual process,
one by one dismissing
the graceful decorations
that dangle from its boughs.

Don't get me wrong.
I welcome the infusion of peek-a-boo sunlight
on fire-red fall foliage.
Sprinkled nearby,
some wildly colored
snapdragons, marigolds, pansies and Asian lilies
peddle their season-ending wares.
And there's an undeterred troop of chirping chickadees
valiantly chasing the warm sun
on those crimson-coated branches.

Alas, I smile sadly and watch
as gold and amber
scarlet and burgundy
abandon my tree limbs,
exit my porch,
vacate my yard.
An army of deserters,
they march down my street
pursued by a fierce autumn wind.

They skip and scoot and scatter and sigh,
whispering their departure with percussionist harmony...

winter is coming
winter is coming

⛤

Rotten Tomatoes

Life on the farm included growing a good-sized garden every year. It was always a family affair of seeding, weeding, irrigating, and rototilling. Personally, my least favorite part was the rototilling. It was always my job to hold back the stems and leaves of the larger plants. I was pretty sure I was going to get a finger whacked off by one of those blades. But truly all of it was hard work and required an ongoing series of tasks, all of which were necessary to preserve our many vegetables. Rows and rows of peppers and potatoes and corn and carrots and cabbage and cantaloupe and beans and beets.

And tomatoes. Tomatoes always did pretty well in our garden, in spite of the short growing season. But at the first sign of frost, we would pull up those plants and drag them down into an unfinished room in our basement, where we hoisted them upside down to hang from the rafters. The tomatoes continued to ripen in this cool, dark space and we could pluck them as needed for quite some time. My parents learned quickly the value of spreading out old newspapers under the plants, since many a tomato made the plunge and the splat, whenever we didn't harvest them in time.

One year, as we were all engaged in a much-needed day of spring cleaning in the basement, we discovered that somehow an errant newspaper splattered with dry, rotten, shriveled-up tomatoes had survived the winter on the floor of our unused room. When mom reached down to dispose of it, my brother suddenly shouted, "No, wait, let me have it."

You have to understand that even from his early years, my brother was a uniquely talented and creative artist. When we were all pretty young, my parents had decided to honor us as children by celebrating a yearly made-up holiday called "Kids Day". We each got to pick the day and the activity. My sister and I would choose picnics, trail rides, going to see a movie, swimming in the nearby Hot Spring pools, things like that. My brother always chose the dump. Yep. As a child, he would rather spend a day at the dump looking for trash he could turn into treasure than just about anything else. He saw potential beauty in things the rest of us deemed totally worthless.

So with our mom's reluctant permission he took that dry, crusty newspaper shrouded in decaying tomatoes, and covered it with some clear coat spray. He crowned it with a homemade, wooden frame and entered it in the county fair. My brother's rotten tomato art got a purple ribbon. Not kidding.

Now isn't that what our incredibly creative God does?

Recognizing in us a potential beauty that others cannot see, He takes our hardened soul with a decaying heart, a heart which the world has labeled as worthless, and pulls us up out of our dark, forgotten, unfinished life. He puts a new frame around that life, crowning us with beauty instead of ashes (Isaiah 61:3) and clothing us in purple as children of Royalty.

We are His proud possession; His most valued, prized creation.

> *"He chose to give birth to us... And we, out of all creation, became His prized possession." – James 1:18 (NLT)*

> *"Therefore, if anyone is in Christ, he is a new creation: The old has gone, the new has come!" – 2 Corinthians 5:17*

> *"I will give you a new heart and put a new Spirit in you; I will remove from you your heart of stone and give you a heart of flesh." – Ezekiel 36:26*

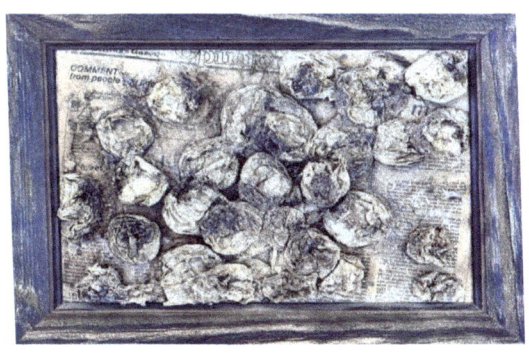

OCTOBER 10.1

Nine Ladies

It's three a.m. and I should be asleep, but my brain keeps telling me that sleeping can wait. These unrelenting thoughts demand a scribe, as they stubbornly shout *write it down!*

I have no choice but to comply. There are nine of us. Not an even number or a round number or a big number, but certainly whole. Definitely complete. Unquestionably perfect. It's an odd number, nine. As are we. Odd, different, a motley crew, with childhoods and backgrounds of function and disfunction. Thrown together through layers of learning, mentoring, sharing, questioning and stretching – a cascade of accountability, encouragement, discipleship and friendship.

We share a past. We have *history*…a rich history. A mosaic of Bible studies and sleepovers and hot tubbing and laughter and pranks and memorizing Scripture and late nights and parties and songs and prayers. We have lived together through hurts and pains and joys and marriages and kids. Oh, the kids. There are adopted kids, step kids, married kids, military kids, grandkids, lots of kids and no kids. We have fought together through doubts and diseases, battles and break-ups, fears and funerals. But in all of it, we continue to experience God's presence, His sovereignty, His victory. In Him we are strong. We are prepared. We are ready.

Once a year we share a house, a weekend, a bathroom, a meal, a couch. We're nurses and teachers and moms and first responders and wives and sisters and friends. There's Betty Jo, our prayer warrior. No doubt words like *grit, determination,* and *tenacity* were invented by authors observing her life. Next to her on that couch, sits Deb in her cozy flannel pants. With a ready smile and infectious laughter, she effortlessly makes us all feel confident, comfortable, content and valued. Standing nearby, MariAnn waits, Bible in hand, passionately eager to share the beauty of Scripture and love of Jesus with all who will listen. There is Amy, ridiculously funny Amy, who is real and vulnerable and quick to strip away any layers made of pretense or posers. Nancy Jo is a creative and gifted planner with a mama bear's protective heart. She hurts when others hurt, comes when others call, and speaks wisdom into the lives of those who are blessed to be near her. Kristin, ever the giver, shares her home, her heart. Not one to linger in the shallow, she knows how deep God's desire is to intercede in our lives through prayer. And Wanda, quiet and aproned in the kitchen, always thinking of others' needs first – not only with her talent of feeding, but always caring, always gifting. Finally, there's Shana, the consummate truth teller who fiercely studies God's Word and is zealous in teaching it. These friends are mine and I am theirs and we belong.

Yes, we have a past. But we also have a present. And that is what makes us unique, I think. Though we've weathered tough storms and broken hearts and fallen friends, yet we remain. We continue to pray and share and give and trust. We laugh, we cry and we hug when we hurt. We congregate, collaborate, communicate. We are more than conquerors. We are iron sharpening iron. We are a chosen people, a royal sisterhood.

And most importantly, we share a future. It is our legacy and it looks like this: We will always pray and support and encourage and pray and love and hope and pray. We're ready. We're ready. *We're ready.*

"Let us not giving up meeting together, as some are in the habit of doing, but let us encourage one another—and all the more as you see the Day approaching." – Hebrews 10:25

10.2
Self-Control & Stress, Part 1: *The Paradox*

Romans 9:16 states, *"It does not, therefore, depend on man's desire or effort, but on God's mercy."* This should be a very freeing verse, reminding us that nothing will ever depend on us and our strivings. All things, always and forever depend on God alone. But since it is within our nature to crave control, we often have a hard time recognizing the *freeing* part. We all struggle for control in our lives. If we can convince ourselves that our desires and efforts will produce results, we tend to feel more powerful and in charge.

Many years ago, someone placed a short article on this issue of wanting control in my mailbox at work. One of the statements caught my eye, and is worth repeating here. *Nothing drains your natural energy supply more than the time, tension, and effort you give to issues in your life over which you have absolutely no control.* How true! What was *not* discussed in the article, but must be understood and embraced, is the realization that there is blessed little in this world over which we *do* have control. The freedom in verse 16 above comes from accepting God's control. Psalm 115:3 states that the Lord can do as He pleases. When we finally choose to surrender all self-effort, we will also naturally surrender the stress, anxiety, and possibly even depression, that often accompany our attempts to run our own lives (and maybe some others?).

Self-control is the final trait listed as part of the nine fruits of the Spirit in Galatians 5:22-23. In some ways, it could potentially be seen as the greatest fruit of all, since it successfully combats all acts of the flesh mentioned in the verses immediately prior (vv.19-21). We should actually be thankful that this battle for control – this conflict with "self" (our flesh) – naturally exists, because it draws us toward God and His Holy Spirit. In Him, we've been given the freedom to relinquish control of self and its fleshly desires, pressing in to the Lord and depending on His power to guide our choices.

God wants to use our lives for His purpose, and He will, if you believe Romans 9:20-21. But a source of great tension is revealed in verse 20: *"Shall what is formed say to Him Who formed it, 'Why did You make me like this?'"* Many of our worries and frustrations come from the unending and pointless "why" questions we are always asking. *Why is this happening to me? Why now? Why is it always me? Why am I so (fat, ugly, messed up, lonely, scared, dumb, different, poor...) Why can't things go right for once? Why is life so difficult?* It seems to me that even these futile questions demonstrate a strong desire for self to be in control.

Self-control is addressed many times in Scripture. Clearly it is something we're expected to understand and experience. Yet when we try to exhibit *self*-control, we always seem to struggle, stress out, and fall short. It's quite possible that self-control is one of those conditions in the Bible which appear to be paradoxical in nature. Other biblical examples include:

- √ the *last* will be *first*
- √ to *lead* others, you must *serve* them
- √ the key to *getting* is *giving*
- √ you have to *die* in order to *live*
- √ you must be a *slave* to be *free*
- √ when you are *weak,* you are *strong*
- √ you can *rise up* only if you *fall*
- √ to be *exalted*, live a life of *humility*
- √ you must be *broken* to be *healed*
- √ *victory* comes through *surrender*

Wouldn't it be appropriate to add *self-control* to this list? I firmly believe that in order to gain any true measure of self-control, we must first be willing to give up the control of self. If you totally surrender control of yourself to God, you may finally experience victory in the area of self-control!

"But you are not controlled by your sinful nature. You are controlled by the Spirit if you have the Spirit of God living in you..." – Romans 8:9a (NLT)

10.3 ☙ ❧

Self-Control & Stress, Part 2: *How To Quit Smoking*

"I've been under a lot of stress lately."
"That job was too stressful, so I just quit."
"All my responsibilities are really stressing me out."

These are familiar statements to most of us. I wonder how much of our stress in life finds its origin in a perceived need to be in control. In part one of this topic, it was noted how ineffective we tend to be at trying to demonstrate self-control. The paradox of achieving success in this area by giving over control of self to God, bears a little further thought.

My parents were both smokers in their young adult years. I asked my mom once how she had managed to quit smoking. By the way, whenever I asked my dad this question, his reply was always the same, "It's easy to quit smoking. I've done it dozens of times!" My mother responded much more seriously, and in a way that brings to light what authentic self-control is all about. She noted that prior to the successful experience which put smoking forever behind her, she had tried many times to quit. She had even, as she put it, "given it up to God" on several occasions. But she failed every time. This particular day, however, was different. My mom explained to me that this time she finally gave it *over* to God. "I don't even know how to tell you what I mean by that," she said.

But I think I know the difference. The other times, when she had given it *up* to the Lord, she would still attempt to control the situation by telling God how best to make it work. There was no true surrender. On this pivotal day, however, she had at last come to realize that she could not handle it herself. So what she really gave *over* to the Lord was the control of self. This submission led to the first true self-control she'd ever experienced in this area. With the issue at last completely and securely in God's hands, change immediately began to happen. That same day, far away on a hunting trip, my dad took one final drag on his own cigarette and said, "No more!"

That was over forty years ago. Neither one of them ever looked back. When we forfeit control to God, things start to change. I recently heard an appropriate quote that was given to a friend of mine by his pastor (unfortunately the original source is unknown). "If you TAKE your problems to the Lord, that is natural; if you GIVE them to the Lord, that is spiritual." We seem to *take* many things to God and then conveniently forget to *give* them over to Him. Why not try taking the step to surrender control of your unmanageable stress and anxiety to the Lord? If you truly release your hold on it, allowing God to completely reign in this area, you will begin experiencing authentic, biblical self-control.

This idea really makes sense when you stop to realize that our sovereign God is always in control anyway. Surely it seems unreasonable to spend your entire life fighting against the Creator of the universe in a battle with a predetermined outcome! This in itself is bound to be a stressful way to live. Remember the old saying to *let go and let God*? That simple, somewhat cheesy sounding platitude is actually rather profound, and certainly difficult to implement.

But maybe we ought to try.

"A man without self-control is like a city broken into and left without walls." – Proverbs 25:28 (ESV)

10.4 ॐ ☙

Self-Control & Stress, Part 3: *Looking at Titus*

The book of Titus contains the most concentrated passage about self-control. There are five different verses containing the Greek words *egkrates* or *sophron*, both of which can be translated as meaning self-control (see ESV or NIV84). In Titus 1:8, Paul notes that elders or overseers are to be *self-controlled*, upright, holy, disciplined. He goes on in chapter two with several more lists of attributes – each of which include self-control – making it clear that this quality is expected not only for overseers, but for the older men (v. 2) and young men (v. 6), as well as both the older and younger women (vv. 3-5). Finally, Paul reminds his readers in verses 11-12 that this trait is attributed to us only by God's grace, not by our own effort. If we surrender to God's control, His salvation and grace will allow us to *"live self-controlled, upright and godly lives in this present age"* (Titus 2:12).

At this point you might be looking for a stronger link between self-control and stress. It's there, I promise. The first half of Titus 2:12 instructs us to say no to the things of this world. I don't know about you, but I can easily get sucked into following the world's priorities. When I peel away the layers, this is almost always what is causing an abundance of stress to take up residence in my day. Striving to control those worldly desires produces anxiety, and inevitably leads to the need for more striving… simply to control my stress level! Yet if I choose instead to recognize God's grace and the Holy Spirit at work in me, with the supernatural power to successfully control my ungodly passions, I won't feel the need to put stress in the driver's seat as I attempt to navigate this life.

My niece's experience in high school was very stressful. She was constantly slammed with over-the-top homework, papers, assignments, and projects required by the charter school where she attended. And at the same time, she was already taking college credit classes. One day, during her junior year, God directed Lizzy to a very enlightening, stress-related Bible passage. She sent me a quick text to share what the Lord was teaching her. How perfectly appropriate that the Scripture Lizzy was drawn to can be found in the very next chapter of Titus. With her permission, here is Lizzy's text:

> I found my own personal stress verses a few days ago. Titus 3:4-8. I love *"stress these things"* – the love and kindness from our Savior – that He saved us because of His mercy and grace, giving us a sure hope in eternal life spent with Him and that it is absolute truth! By stressing THESE things, the things that matter, we may be careful to devote ourselves to doing good, not stressing work or homework or school or chores or taxes. Stress THESE things! It's a good reminder for me, and gives me peace and refocus.

Like my niece, most of us typically find ourselves getting completely stressed over the wrong things, things in our daily lives that we have very little ability to control. A consistent pattern of giving over that control to the Lord allows us the freedom to *stress* the right things. The word translated as "stress" in this verse means to affirm strongly, to assert confidently. We are to strongly affirm and confidently assert the good things declared in God's Word… such as His ever-present kindness, love and mercy, His miraculous gift of salvation and renewal by the Holy Spirit, and the incredible hope of eternal life! Can I hear an amen?

"But when the kindness and love of God our Savior appeared, He saved us, not because of righteous things we had done, but because of His mercy. He saved us… by the Holy Spirit, Whom He poured out on us generously through Jesus Christ our Savior, so that, having been justified by His grace, we might become heirs having the hope of eternal life…I want you to ***stress these things****, so that those who have trusted in God may be careful to devote themselves to doing what is good. These things are excellent and profitable…"* – Titus 3:4-8 *(bold added)*

NOVEMBER 11.1

Not to Worry

Question. Is worrying or being stressed a sin? It certainly behaves like one. Note these traits: It leads to poor choices, keeps us from doing God's will by distracting us and clouding our judgment, can be habit forming, makes us feel guilty, negates God's control and leaves room for Satan's influence. Most importantly, we are told many times in Scripture <u>not</u> to *worry* or *be anxious* (Phil. 4:6, Ps. 37:1, Mt. 6:25). So even if we refuse to label our anxiety as sin, could we still treat it as such and choose not to live in it any longer (Rom. 6:2)?

Theoretically, yes. Yet when it comes to the moment of choice, we often find ourselves in the situation Paul tackles in Romans 7. He notes, *"...what I want to do I do not do, but what I hate I do"* (v. 15). We can tell ourselves not to get stressed out about something, but anxiety is often still present despite the desire to eliminate it. Interestingly, this seeming inability to make the firm choice of not giving in to worry is simply one more behavioral similarity to sin.

When I decided to pursue a master's degree, I applied to seven different schools. Which I don't recommend to anyone. Way too many decisions, forms, paperwork and frustration. Especially if you get accepted to all seven. Or if you get multiple scholarship offers. How do you ever determine the best one? Lots and lots of prayer, I guess. Which ultimately, is what led me to Ball State University. The farthest away, the least prestigious, and the only school where I knew absolutely no one. These things definitely concerned me, but despite my worries, I knew with certainty that God was sending me there. So I flew out to Muncie, Indiana for a look-see. The head of the department, a rather tall and imposing man named Dr. Hoops, took me around on an informal campus tour. He only asked me one question: "Why did you decide to come *here*?"

I am certain my answer was far from what he expected.

"I'm not really sure. All I know is this is where God called me to be." His reaction was simply to change the subject.

I didn't really interact with Dr. Hoops again during my tenure at Ball State. He was an audiology professor, and since my degree was in speech/language pathology, I never took a class from him and rarely saw him even from a distance. Fast forward two years. One day I happened to be walking in the hallway when Dr. Hoops was passing through. He stopped.

"So, do you still believe that God called you here?"

I definitely did. Maybe one reason was to help me clearly see the lasting impact that a simple two-sentence conversation could have on someone who was pretty much a stranger. I learned a lot of other impactful things during my stay in Muncie. And one of my greatest ah-ha moments about stress and worry actually came via a different professor. In class, he once rattled off his personal definition of worry – which, by the way, has been much more memorable to me over time than any academic information he ever shared. Not a Christian, as far as I could tell, he still had an unusual awareness of the spiritual consequences of fretting. "Worry," he stated, "is the sinful misuse of God's gift of creativity." Quite an insightful observation, I think. Isn't it true that much of our struggle with stress comes from a God-given ability to create and imagine all manner of future scenarios, only to begin obsessing on every potential problem or failure? Hmmm.

"...they are choked with worries and riches and pleasures of this life, and bring no fruit to maturity." – Luke 8:14 (NASB)

"And if worry can't accomplish a little thing... what's the use of worrying over bigger things?" – Luke 12:26 (NLT)

11.2

Aarons and Hurs

This is an uncomfortable story for me. But it's an important one, revealing incredible aspects of God's character, His design for prayer, and the value of community. Here goes…

When I was in my twenties, I got dumped after a four-year relationship that I truly thought would end in marriage. I was devastated. Thus began a steep downhill ride on a fun-free rollercoaster, that wouldn't truly be over for about three years. The beginning was the worst of it, of course. I spent many evenings on the floor of my kitchen with a box of tissues. Winters were hardest, as I developed a form of seasonal depression. The cold, the wind, the dark, the loneliness. Every fall, I began dreading the next four months. The expectation of misery was in itself very discouraging. I became so downcast in my soul, I couldn't even continue to pray about it anymore.

One evening a friend showed up at my door. This particular day had actually been a really good one for me, surprisingly free of my unwanted emotional houseguests.

"Here, I brought you this." She handed me a plaque with a Bible verse. "God put you on my mind five times today and I've been praying." MariAnn knew nothing of the major hurt in my heart, but it was obvious God had used her prayers to bless and encourage me with a spiritually uplifting day.

On a morning not too long after that, I started off my workday with such a discouraged spirit and heavy heart that I wasn't certain I could accomplish my job responsibilities. I called a friend at his workplace and asked him to please pray for me when he got a minute. About an hour later, all of my oppressive, overwhelming feelings of despair were suddenly gone. I called my friend a second time. I thought I already knew the answer, but I had to ask: "Have you had a chance to pray for me yet?"

"I actually did it just now!" he chuckled.

I knew that. I mean, I didn't know, but I *knew*. And there

were several more after these two experiences, where I could tell that someone out there was praying for me. Beautiful days. Pain free days. But God had yet to show me the *how* and *why*.

That spring, I took some college students to a retreat. The man who had been a mentor to me since my own college days was there. Dave always carved out time to meet with me, answer my abundant questions, and teach me something new. Although he was unaware of my currently less-than-wonderful mental state, his words were surprisingly perfect.

"There's a story in Exodus where Joshua fought an enemy, the Amalekites (Ex. 17:9-13), overcoming them because of Moses, Aaron and Hur. Those three went to the top of a hill and Moses stood with the staff of God in his hands. As long as Moses held up his hands, the Israelites were winning in battle, but whenever he lowered his hands, they were losing. When Moses' hands grew tired, Aaron and Hur held his hands up— one on each side—so that his hands remained steady. I believe there are times in life when we're too exhausted, too burdened by the battle in front of us, and we haven't the strength to lift our hands up in prayer. This is when God provides others, our 'Aarons and Hurs', to lift our arms up for us, petitioning Him on our behalf. This is how we overcome the enemy *together*."

Wow, what timely words. Dave had no way of knowing how my intimate Father was revealing Himself to me at that moment. The Lord had been providing His lonely, discouraged daughter with some Aarons and Hurs, comrade prayer warriors to stand by my side and fight this battle with me.

At last, one winter the expected depression didn't happen. No more tears. No more lonely nights on the kitchen floor. No oppressive feelings of hopelessness. They were gone, replaced with a comforting sense of normalcy. I credit that change to some anonymous prayer warrior. Or maybe more than one, prompted by the Holy Spirit to come along side, to lift up their weary fellow believer's arms in prayer.

This is how we overcome.

"... pray for each other so that you may be healed. The prayer of a righteous person is powerful and effective." – James 5:16

11.3

Bringing Candy

I never had kids of my own. Dave and I got married a little later in life. We both prayerfully decided because of that fact, and with all the kids we were responsible for in our college ministry, plus all the children I was responsible for in the school where I worked, it made sense to stay DINKs (you know, Double Income No Kids). Therefore, I have instead chosen to dote exceedingly on all my nieces and nephews. I love each one of them with all my heart and I really want them to know that.

The first three were born when I was still single. While they were young, I used to bring them gifts, candy, or some kind of treat every time I went to see them. On each visit, I told them the same story… how when I was little, my uncle Raymond would never fail to bring chocolate whenever he came to see us. Not once did I doubt that he loved my siblings and me, because he always thought of us before coming and made sure he had yummy treats ready to give us every single time. Uncle Raymond was my favorite, and it wasn't really because of the candy so much as the underlying message that he loved me dearly.

As soon as I became an aunt, I resolved to echo that tradition. On every visit to my little buddies, I would hand over their tasty treasures with loving enthusiasm and repeat my customary question:

"Why do I bring you goodies?"

I'm sure it got old. They would roll their eyes and give a big sigh, but then faithfully reply that since I always knew my uncle thought of me ahead of time because he loved me so much, this gift was a reminder of how much I loved them and how often I thought of them even when we were apart.

One such conversation with my four-year-old niece Charlie resulted in a humorous anecdote that I've shared for many years now and makes me laugh with every telling. As I placed in her hands a small bag of chocolate treats, I made my usual query, "Why did I bring you this candy?"

"Because you love me."

I smiled and nodded, "Yes, Charlie, that's my reason."

Then she added proudly, "And I love *you* because you bring me candy, *too!*" Oh, the honest reasoning of a child.

I sometimes wonder if this same juvenile mentality is ever at the heart of my response to the riches God has bestowed on me. He brings me gifts and blessings and answers to prayer, just wanting me to truly grasp how much it is that He loves me. Do I reciprocate with the same benevolent and altruistic devotion toward my Lord? Or is it really more along the lines of, *and I love You too because You give me what I want...*

The greatest commandment, according to Christ's own words in Mark 12:30, is an instruction for believers to *"Love the Lord your God with all your heart and with all your soul and with all your mind and with all your strength."*

Please take note that nowhere in Scripture are we told do this because He brings us gifts.

"We love because He first loved us." – 1 John 4:19

who am i, and who are my people, that we should be able to give as generously as this? EVERYTHING comes from you and we have given you only what comes from Your hand.
– I Chronicles 29:14

11.4

Receive the Bumps

One thing I have noticed in this life is that most of us tend to spend a good chunk of our available energy trying unsuccessfully to eliminate all the things that might trigger discouragement, pain, fear, grief or anxiety. Yet, those same stressors are as much a normal part of life as all the positives.

I Peter 5:7 says we are to cast all of our worries, our unmet desires and failed expectations on God Himself. Because He will certainly get rid of them, right? He will make it all go away, yes? Not what the verse says. It says: *because God cares for you.* He gets it. He understands better than anyone how beautiful the perfect life can be. Will be. But He also understands that it won't happen this side of eternity. We are currently living in the disappointment gap, that place between two perfect gardens. And without a doubt, we will have pain and sorrow and a balancing lump of negatives that aren't going to go away. Expending all of our effort and energy trying to eradicate them will just increase our anxiety.

In Luke 22:31-32 we learn that Jesus prayed for Simon Peter, who was going to go through a "sifting" by Satan. During this experience, he would actually deny his personal relationship with Christ. Sounds incredibly negative and anxiety-producing to me. But Jesus assured Peter both before and after the incident that He would never desert him. Christ also prayed for him: *"Simon, Simon, Satan has asked to sift you as wheat. But I have prayed for you, Simon, that your faith may not fail..."* Jesus didn't petition for removal from the circumstances, He simply prayed that Simon Peter's faith would not fail. The Lord is unquestionably on our side in difficult situations, but His intent is to walk with us *through* our trials, not help us find a way to *avoid* them.

When Dave and I were in Hawaii, we had the exciting and unexpected pleasure of going on a helicopter tour over the magnificent mountains of Kauai. Neither of us had ever been in a helicopter before. It was open-air, no doors, and can I say, very, very bouncy. I am extremely afraid of flying, so I naturally had lots of anxiety about the turbulence. But the pilot was wonderful. He spoke into our head phones in a calm, soothing voice, telling us that those jolts and jerks were very natural – a normal, much expected part of the experience.

"Just receive the bumps," he reassured us. "Take them in, accept them." He said it several times and I believed him. He was, after all, knowledgeable and capable and in control. His honest words were a comfort and encouragement, allowing me to embrace all of those unpleasant bumps and enjoy some of the most stunning, incredible panoramas in all creation.

God is the Pilot of my life. He is in control. And I'm pretty sure He's telling me just to receive all my anxiety-producing bumps, to bring them in and accept them as a normal, expected part of the turbulent ride called life.

"Say to those with anxious heart, 'Take courage, fear not. Behold, your God will come… He will save you.'"
  – Isaiah 35:4 (NASB)

* Anxiety is a frequent flyer in the head space of many folks these days. Do you experience it quite often or know of someone who struggles with a lot of anxiety? What are some of your favorite verses to battle these unwanted fears? Can you write out a prayer to the Lord, petitioning Him to help you and/or your friend?

Verses:
_____
_____
_____
_____

Prayer:
_____
_____
_____
_____
_____
_____
_____
_____
_____
_____
_____
_____
_____
_____
_____
_____

DECEMBER

It was early in December, many years ago. First semester of freshman year, I do believe. There I sat, at my dorm room desk. Sullen and hunched over – a desperate and blatant procrastinator – with text books sprawled out as I reluctantly engaged in some last-minute cramming for finals. And all the while, staring out at the pile of fresh snow silently collecting on my window sill...

Prisoner

The snow falls soft
against my window pane,
making noises
only the deaf could hear;
while the vague reflection
looking back at me,
wonders why
I stop to shed a tear.

And will never know
that I cry because,
those flakes of white
seem very near —
Yet fall so freely
right outside
While I am definitely
stuck in here.

* Does this time of year inspire you to be creative? Go out to your shop and build something sturdy? Head to your kitchen and bake something delicious? Cozy up on your couch and write something interesting? God made each of us creative in different ways.

Have you ever tried writing a poem? Use the space below and let your creative juices come to life in this season. I bet no one's ever written a poem about shoveling sidewalks or driving around to look at Christmas lights or finding joy when it's cold and windy outside. Be the first.

Or maybe just use this space to make a list of people you need to creatively connect with this December.

Then do it.

12.1

Joy or Happiness?

Not long ago, I was remembering a few lines from a poem I had read back in my teenage years: "I believe in the sun even when it's not shining... and I believe in God, even when He is silent." This was apparently written during World War II, on the wall of a cellar in a Cologne concentration camp, by an unknown Jewish prisoner.

These simple words of faith got me to thinking. Do I often depend on circumstances to validate the presence of joy in my life or can I still believe – can I trust God – even when I am not experiencing any confirmation physically or emotionally? I know that many people use the words *joy* and *happiness* interchangeably. But it seems to me there is quite a bit of difference. I think it is definitely possible to be happy about something without experiencing any true joy. Likewise, I have found that I can actually be full of joy even at times when I don't gain the things which might have made me happy. The experience of happiness appears to be contingent upon positive circumstances. Joy, on the other hand, can be present even in the midst of unpleasant situations.

One December evening I was in my kitchen preparing dinner. I had turned the television on for some background noise while cooking. My attention was drawn to the last few seconds of an advertisement which was apparently promoting some type of credit card. The gist of the commercial was that we should all buy better gifts for Christmas that year. I must admit that I get quite annoyed with advertisers who attempt to hijack a God-honoring holiday in order to make money. But the frustrating thing that really caught my attention this time was the company tagline at the end of the commercial. It said: *You. Me. Happier*.

There goes the prevailing secular culture, I thought, trying to package and market our happiness. Isn't it interesting? The clear assumption is that we all desire to be, and somehow need to be, happier. And that this will come about if we buy more and better stuff. Whenever we desperately crave or long for something more, we are in effect expressing discontentment and dissatisfaction with our current state. Consider this quote: "Happiness is what you feel when you can have whatever it is that you want. Joy is what you learn when you can *want* whatever it is that you *have*."

In any contest, discontent will always fight to get the upper hand. It is the big bully on the playground and will show up strong in a battle against joy. Whereas, a contented heart will become your toughest ally, advocating and inspiring great joy. Contentment begins to take root when we resist the tantalizing voice that whispers, "I need more." It is a fundamental truth that real satisfaction is sustainable only through unfettered trust in what the Lord has already provided. And the requisite byproduct will be joy! Dissatisfaction steals joy from us and replaces it with a perpetual quest for more comfort, quicker gratification and greater pleasure. *you. me. happier?* Maybe. *Joyful?* Not so much.

"Satisfy us in the morning with Your unfailing love, that we may sing for joy and be glad all our days." – Psalm 90:14

"Provide for those who grieve in Zion—to bestow on them a crown of beauty instead of ashes, the oil of joy instead of mourning, and a garment of praise instead of a spirit of despair..." – Isaiah 61:3

* When have you experienced joy in the midst of imperfect circumstances?

_____
_____
_____
_____
_____
_____
_____

12.2

Sunsets, Part 1: *He Knows, He Cares*

The final few years of my mother's life were difficult for me. I was the primary care provider while still trying to let her stay in her own place for as long as possible. I went over there every day after work. Whenever I wasn't there, she would constantly call me on the phone about something. One evening my husband and I stopped to see her on our way to Bible study. I left her with the TV turned on to a show she liked to watch. Barely two minutes after we drove off, my phone rang.

"My television won't turn on." There was no use arguing that I had just set it up moments before.

"Okay Mom, I'll be right over." So frustrating. I dropped my husband off where we were meeting for Bible study and promised to be back as soon as possible. During the short time it took to return to my mom's, the phone rang twice more. First, my brother calling from Colorado.

"Hey, Mom just called. She needs help with her TV." Even though it wasn't his fault, I replied in a very irritated voice that I was already on my way over there to take care of it. I hung up and immediately my cell rang again. This time it was our college ministry intern letting me know that one of my students had just broken up with her boyfriend and was pretty distraught about it.

"Okay, I'll call her." By now, I was starting to feel very overwhelmed and telling God, *I can't do this!* After turning mom's TV on a second time and reminding her where the on/off button on the remote was, I headed back out to the car. I was so weary. My phone rang for a third time. It was the boyfriend. "You better call Brittney. We just broke up and she's not doing so well."

Okay, okay, okay. Completely frustrated and discouraged by now, with two crises and way late for Bible study, I started crying as I drove back. *I mean it, God. I can't do this!*

Suddenly I became aware of something unusual, ultimately impossible. I realized that the entire time I had been dealing with all of this, I had been staring at the most beautiful sunset. This means that for about fifteen solid minutes, while driving in four different directions, God had provided a spectacular view of His colorful palette. I'm not trying to say this was some weirdly miraculous occurrence – maybe I saw some of it in my side or rearview mirrors, and partial cloud cover could have made it last longer. But the fact remains that this fantastic sunset was there in front of me, and for the majority of the experience I was totally missing it, except maybe on some subconscious level. It was like God had been saying, *I hear you, I'm with you, now look what I have for you…*

I can't do this!

I know, child. I get it. But c'mon now, can't you see? There is beauty here in the midst of your pain and I am with you through all of it. What a splendid message of comfort and reassurance; God's healing peace in its purest form.

On many occasions since, I've felt a similar crushing sense of failure as I try to navigate life and various responsibilities. I find myself saying *God, I need a sunset now.* He never fails to respond. But I have to say, it isn't always an actual sunset.

Once, while sobbing my way back out to my car after a particularly stressful evening at my mother's, there in the night sky was a gloriously bright supermoon, my promise of His presence. Another time, after a frantic phone call at about 11:30 p.m., I jumped in my car and headed to mom's again, streaming familiar tears and repeating my new mantra: *God, I need a sunset!* At that moment, a magnificent antlered deer strutted across the street in front of me and bounded off into the darkness. *Wow. Thank You, Lord.*

I am with you. All the time. Believe it.

"…I am with you always, to the very end of the age." – Mt. 28:20

"At sunset, the people brought to Jesus all who had various kinds of sickness, and laying His hands on each one, He healed them." – Luke 4:40

12.3

Sunsets, Part 2: *Retirement Choices*

I will refrain from overwhelming you with all of my sunset stories, but there is one more which must be shared. One instance that could never be explained away as simple coincidence.

Not too long ago, I was finally ready to consider closing out my career as a speech/language pathologist for the school district. They were offering incentives to retire early, so my husband and I started praying about whether I should work one more year or not. I didn't tell him this, but I also prayed that God might show me which of these to do, by His response to a second prayer. My husband is in fulltime college ministry, making his living through the financial and prayer support of partners with a passion for funding that kind of ministry. His financial support had recently dipped somewhat, so my prayer was as follows: *God if you want me to retire this year, please raise up one more ministry partner for Dave. If not, I will continue to work another year.*

Some might consider this bargaining with God, but I felt like it would be a prayerful way to be certain about the Lord's direction on my retirement timeline. The reason I didn't tell my husband about this aspect of my prayer was because I didn't want him feeling pressured to try and raise more support just so I might not have to work longer.

We prayed for several months. When the deadline for submitting my desired end-date was only a few days away, I asked Dave if he'd gained any new supporters recently. Nope.

I now had my answer. I would be working one more year.

I set a meeting with the HR department for the next day, asking if I might come over at 4:00. They said to show up at 4:30, which turned out to be significant. As I drove to my appointment, it occurred to me for the first time that I was really basing this important decision on the complete absence of an observable answer. If God had provided an additional ministry partner, it would be a clear sign that He was answering my prayer. But I had set myself up to accept silence as an indication of the other choice. I had to laugh at this, while at the same time try to deal with some unexpected doubts about whether this silence actually was an answer from God. I mean, maybe it was just silence. My sudden misgivings were a bit overwhelming, creating some hesitation and stress. I prayed fervently as I walked in the building. *Lord, I'm trusting that Your lack of a sign is in response to my prayer and I'm going to step out in faith that I'm doing the right thing here!*

After signing the papers confirming my commitment to one additional year with the district, I headed outside to my car. And there it was. Filling the entire expanse of the sky – the most brilliant, incredible sunset! From the western side clear over to the east, magnificent clouds reflected the sun's rays in a palette of red and pink and orange and yellow. It was so gloriously extraordinary that I grabbed my phone and took a panoramic photo to send to my husband. If I had gone at 4:00 like I'd originally planned, I would have missed it.

You were hoping for a sign? Well, let Me reward your little step of faith with undeniable evidence – by painting My evening sky in a splendidly vivid and obvious answer!

Now, whenever I notice my friends in their own stressful and uncertain circumstances, I tell them. I tell them to ask God for a sunset. Oh, the stories and pictures they've shared with me over the years, as God comes through once again, always providing His calming peace, His healing hope.

"They who dwell at the ends of the earth stand in awe of Your signs; You make the sunrise and the sunset shout for joy."
– Psalm 65:8 (NASB)

12.4

Rain at Christmas

Sometimes you just have to laugh. We all appreciate a person with a great sense of humor. And I'm pretty sure our Creator God has the best one of all.

It was about a week before Christmas and I had just come home from college on semester break. My father was on the phone with an elder from a tiny church in a nearby town where he had been asked to preach in a few days. Manderson was a rural smattering of perhaps a hundred people, only nine miles from our ranch. When he hung up the phone, dad immediately came and found me.

"Sorry to interrupt your reading, but the lady who plays piano at the church is sick. I'm wondering if you'd be willing to lead the congregation in a couple of Christmas carols."

During my teen years, I had taken piano lessons for about a year and a half. I like to think that if I had kept with it, I might be pretty good. But I'm definitely not.

"No way. I don't play in front of people."

My father tried a few persuasive tactics. "Oh, come on. You play carols for the family every Christmas and you do fine. Besides, the lady they normally have isn't very good either. The congregation won't expect much and they will certainly appreciate anything you are willing to do."

"Nope." I shook my head. "Playing for family is different. You know I don't play in front of people."

"But you would have plenty of time to practice and like I said, nobody cares if it's perfect." He had such a begging look on his face, but I held firm.

"Not gonna happen, dad."

He made one last attempt to influence. "Well maybe you should pray about it tonight. Then when you wake up in the morning, if this is the first thing you think about – well maybe that is God telling you to do it."

My father's sassy, smart-mouthed daughter showed up at this point. "Oh yeah? Why don't I just ask God to make it rain or something!" Dad looked at me for a long minute and shook his head. Then he turned and walked away.

I went back to reading my novel. It was a good one. A few minutes later my dad returned. "Pssst." I reluctantly looked up.

He said nothing, but with a smug look on his face and a crooked finger, he beckoned me to follow him. I put down my book with a loud *'stop bothering me'* sigh, and let him lead the way to the front door of our home.

It would be important at this point to make sure you understand that it never rained in December where I grew up. Never. So my dad pushed open the screen door and pointed to our concrete porch. Which was covered with multiple little round wet spots. It was raining. In Wyoming. In December. Not much or for long, just enough for my father to notice and point it out to me.

I went straight into the living room and sat down at the piano. While I was practicing those carols, I thought about what I had learned. My funny, funny God had used humor to teach me that it is never about skill or perfection or comfort level or talent. It is about willingness and availability and trusting our Father to give us what we need to be successful in the things He asks of us. Pride says, *I can't do this because I might fail or be embarrassed.* Humility says, *with God ALL things are possible; He gives me the strength to do it.* Always remember God will not give us more than HE can handle.

It turns out the church pianist was all better by the time Sunday rolled around, and I didn't have to play after all. I always wondered, though, if listening to me practice for three days made God decide it'd be easier to heal her illness than to make me sound decent. Sometimes you just have to laugh.

"Jesus… said, 'With man this is impossible, but not with God; all things are possible with God.'" – Mark 10:27

"I can do everything through Him Who gives me strength." – Philippians 4:13

WINTER AGAIN

Well, it's back to being winter. We have now come full circle if you've stayed the course and read a weekly story. I always hate for good things to end, and it's been a good thing for me to write this all down – even if no one ever reads it. All that to say, I don't want it to end. I want to connect with you all a little while longer. So, as Paul told the Corinthian believers at the end of his first letter, "Perhaps I will stay with you for a while, or even spend the winter…" (1 Cor. 16:6). Perhaps – if you're willing – I'll stay with you a while longer, at least long enough to share a couple more stories. It's okay. No pressure. Read them at your leisure. Or not at all.

Fresh Off the Cutting Room Floor

#1: Thinkin' About It

My oldest niece now has two children of her own. The first born is named Wyatt. Quite precocious for a three-year-old, his verbal skills have brought the family a lot of laughter already. One day, he was sitting at the kitchen table eating a turkey and cheese wrap sandwich that his mom had made for him. He was about half done munching his way through it, when their dog Murph came up next to him. Murph sat back on his hind legs and stared at Wyatt's sandwich, anxiously begging with his big puppy dog eyes and his tongue hanging out. Wyatt looked at the dog, looked at his half-eaten wrap, back at the dog – seriously pondering the situation. My niece had been standing nearby, watching this scene develop.

Mom: "Don't even think about it!"
Wyatt: "I'm thinkin' about it!"

You see what I mean about the laughter, right? Oh, that kid makes me chuckle. But I have to say, I sure hope our Heavenly Father also has a sense of humor whenever we do pretty much the same thing. Many temptations present themselves to us as we munch our way through life. And it seems we often find it worth pondering the situation. God, through His Word, the Holy Spirit or both, declares: *Not wise – don't even think about it.* At which point, we might be inclined to reply: *I'm still thinking about it!*

There are plenty of reasons to mind that wise Parental command, and even if we can't see it at the time, the potential of a momentary pleasure will never be worth the consequences of not obeying.

So don't even think about it.

"There's a way of life that looks harmless enough; look again... Sure, those people appear to be having a good time, but all that laughter will end in heartbreak." – Proverbs 14:12-13 (MSG)

#2: Never Give Up

One of the most difficult aspects of prayer is exhibiting patience. But sometimes the answers to certain prayers can take a really long time. Thomas Edison is credited as saying, "Our greatest weakness lies in giving up." There will be prayers which don't get answered for many years. So I say to you, keep praying. Never give up.

Now, you might be wondering why I chose an Edison quote to inspire you instead of the famous short speech by Churchill to "never, never give up." Except apparently, he didn't actually say that. And apparently, it wasn't even a very short speech. Do some research. The quote above, however, attributed to Edison, makes a great point. We humans tend toward the weakness of quitting.

Yet there are petitions – which God truly desires to grant – that require great perseverance. God has been known to respond well to tenacity and doggedness. Think of the bold prayers of Abraham as he implored God to save Sodom. The Lord definitely responded to Abraham's persistence in Genesis 18, and was willing to consider amending His judgment on the city. Think of the prayers of Hannah (I Samuel 1), as she struggled with barrenness for so many years. God heeded those prayers also, rewarding her grit and determination with a son named Samuel. In the New Testament, Jesus tells His disciples a couple of parables, both in the book of Luke, which confirm God's desire for us to never give up praying until we receive an answer. One parable is found in chapter 11 and the other is a few chapters later in Luke 18.

The Greek word for "pester" (kopos) shows up in both parables. First, in the neighbor's words, *"don't bother me"* in Luke 11:7 and again when the judge says, *"this widow keeps bothering me"* (Luke 18:5). Both times, the petitioner's boldness results in reward. These twin word-picture parables indicate that persistence is a genuine expression of true faith.

In chapter 11, it is interesting to note that Jesus has just been sharing with His disciples a template for how to pray (v. 2-4). Then immediately after the parable, in verse 9, He makes another famous statement: *"ask and it will be given to you; seek and you will find; knock and the door will be opened..."* And sandwiched there in between, we are taught to pester, to be bold and annoyingly tenacious in prayer. And be patient.

Never. Give. Up.

During my summers, years ago, I would leave for about a month on a mission trip to inner-city Chicago. The first year, I was blessed to share the gospel with a young girl named Camesha, and she accepted Christ. I prayed for Camesha's spiritual growth (in a very difficult culture and area) for many years, even after we were no longer taking teams there on summer trips. 18 years later, we once again took a team of college students to the same place over spring break. I was at last able to reconnect with a now-adult Camesha, who had since gotten married, stayed married, had a good job, and was raising her little boy to love Jesus. God honored that long-term prayer and blessed me to eventually see His clear response.

Recently, the Lord again encouraged me by revealing His firm answer to another pestering prayer of mine. About 10 years ago, a friend shared concerns about some scary, illegal treatment of children that was happening within orphanages in Haiti. It really touched my heart. So I started praying diligently for those little ones; for their health, safety and salvation. Last spring – a decade later – a young lady showed up on campus, came to our ministry, and then joined my discipleship group. I have since found out two amazing things. The first is that Fafane actually grew up in an orphanage in Haiti. Healthy and safe. The second is that she now excitedly declares that her personal relationship with Christ began as a result of what she learned in discipleship group this past year. All those years of praying for orphans whom I thought I would never meet. And then what does God do? He brings Fafane *here*, to my small group, on a pretty small campus in a pretty small town.

I will share two more brief examples of the Lord responding favorably to patient, but determined intercession. One is that for 12 years, I prayed for my brother to get right with the Lord. Then I watched him finally begin to change as the Holy Spirit got ahold of his heart. The other is the 15 years I prayed for a husband. I never gave up. Again, the Lord rewarded my bold persistence – with an impossibly perfect mate. I praise God for teaching me to maintain a shameless tenacity in my prayers.

    I have more. I could go on. But it's time now to stop reminiscing about the past and start praying about the future.

"Never stop praying." – 1 Thessalonians 5:17 (NLT)

"Then Jesus told His disciples a parable to show them that they should always pray and not give up." – Luke 18:1

Camesha – 1993

Camesha – 2011

#3: Kip

Can we learn anything from an Australian Blue Heeler? My childhood dog, Kip, was named after Rudyard Kipling (late 19th century poet and author). I always thought my mom told us it was because they were both Australian, but nope. I have since learned that Mr. Kipling was born in India. Apparently, however, he once visited and wrote about Australia? So that must be the connection. Kip, on the other hand, was born in Wyoming and never once visited Australia.

Loved that dog. And oh, the stories I could tell you, as he entertained our family for many years. Here's just a sample of Kip Life on the farm…

One of his core personality traits was a restless need to protect his kingdom. This included us, our property, and our cats. We were Pack. Everything else was not Pack and should beware. Kip went after pretty much anything that moved fast and made noise. This included cars. He never once killed a car. Never even slowed one down. But it wasn't for lack of trying. And he wore a path through our yard with his relentless pursuits.

I have to confess that my husband does this also. He isn't as committed to the process as his canine counterpart, and they have different motives. Dave's is just a lazy desire to reach the truck quicker on his way to work. Using the sidewalk simply takes too long. Thus, I have a nice, tramped down shortcut across my lawn. But it makes me smile and brings back those Kippy memories.

Kip's motive was his endless, if unmet, desire to take down a vehicle. He wanted to conquer every motorized beast that might threaten his empire. But it wasn't to be. You could look at the worn-out grass trail and figure out why he always failed. The angle was all wrong. He needed to make a sharper cut or start sooner or run faster. Or maybe just choose a different way to do battle.

I sometimes wonder if I am any smarter than a Blue Heeler. I'm often tempted to chase after things I have no business chasing. To try and fight battles that aren't mine to fight. To feel threatened by those I perceive as enemies when maybe they are simply passing by. My focus gets distracted and I take on the role of protector, when my Heavenly Father has already promised to be the One in charge of my safety here within His kingdom. He has the better angle. In fact, my sovereign God is able to see *all* the angles, and He alone can take down my enemies. I need to choose a different way to do battle. I must learn to confine my relentless pursuit to a heavenward petition in prayer whenever I feel threatened.

Kip was a very clever dog who did a lot of smart things in his short life. Chasing after cars wasn't one of them. I am hoping to do a smart thing in my life and chase after the God Who is committed to conquering my enemies for me.

"Do not be afraid of them; the LORD your God Himself will fight for you." – Deuteronomy 3:22

#4: Hannah

My friend Hannah is a fabulous photographer. She is an even better singer and worship leader, but that's a story for another day. I must confess to you that Hannah is far better at sharing the details of this particular God encounter, but I guess you are stuck with my second-hand rendition.

Hannah gets asked to photograph a lot of weddings. Not long ago, she was hired to use her camera and skills to record that very special day for a couple who were getting married in another state. Some of the equipment Hannah needed was rented, so she had it shipped directly to the destination city.

After receiving a heads-up from some other wedding goers who also had to travel, Hannah set out on her trip a day early. In good weather, it was only about a five-hour drive, but this was January. And one of the biggest storms of the season was now brewing. Treacherous roads and multiple highway closures turned her simple trip into a two-day event that included an unexpected hotel stay, but she did finally arrive in time for the rehearsal.

The rented camera accessories did not.

Hannah immediately called UPS and was informed that due to the inclement weather, her shipment was impossibly stuck in another facility along the route. Because several of the rented items were quite vital to the success of her photo shoot plans, Hannah did not receive this information with great joy. Quite the opposite. Not totally panicking yet, but definitely very concerned, she began asking those present to pray for a miracle – that these important items might arrive in time for the festivities. Incredibly, the mail delivery service called Hannah back less than an hour later, to say that her package had somehow reached its destination.

On her way to retrieve the equipment, a jubilant Hannah began singing praises to the Lord, giving thanks to Him, rejoicing in Him, blessing His name, His goodness – grateful for the God of miracles, Who had understood her frustrations and quickly responded.

Her joy and relief, however, was short-lived. When Hannah got back in her car and opened up the package, she realized that only part of the shipment had shown up. Unfortunately, it was not the portion she needed most, and in fact, was quite useless without the other, still truant equipment.

As you can probably imagine, this reality was quite devastating. Hannah had not been feeling very hopeful all weekend anyway, due to her messed-up travel plans… icy highways, road closures, and unanticipated hotel expenses. She now found herself becoming disheartened again and spiraling down emotionally. But it was at this moment when Hannah suddenly felt God speaking very clearly and specifically into her weary, discouraged heart.

Hey Hannah, remember just a few minutes ago, when you were so confidently praising Me for how faithful I am and how good I am? Well, that's still Me. I'm still that good. Still that faithful. Even right now.

Is it possible for you to embrace My unconditional goodness in the midst of your disappointment? Do you recognize My abiding faithfulness even if you're not feeling it? Can you experience My hope when your situation doesn't seem hopeful?

Our intimate and personal God was impressing upon Hannah an unmistakable insight – the ability to grasp something more of His blessed, unchanging character – and experience hope apart from momentary evidence, appreciate His goodness apart from fleeting confirmation. And she resolved to settle there, to camp out in this fundamental truth, even if her current circumstances beckoned a different direction.

In the Message version of the Bible, Eugene Peterson has paraphrased the wording of Job 1:21 in a very clear and succinct way: *"God gives, God takes. God's name be ever blessed."*

Job was able to recognize the same fundamental truth; that no matter what happens, whether I get or whether I don't get, *blessed* be the name of the Lord. Not blessed when... Not blessed if... Not blessed because...

Just *Blessed*.

As I mentioned earlier, Hannah is quite the phenomenal photographer. The pictures turned out beautiful. And if that newlywed couple's friends or family ever have the opportunity to peruse the completed wedding album, all will come away from their experience rightly amazed and praising her talents. Hannah, on the other hand, has come away from her own experience rightly amazed and praising *God*… rejoicing in Him, blessing His good name, and giving thanks in *all* circumstances.

"Though the fig tree does not bud and there are no grapes on the vines, though the olive crop fails and the fields produce no food, though there are no sheep in the pen and no cattle in the stalls, yet I will rejoice in the Lord, I will be joyful in God my Savior." – Habakkuk 3:17-18

"I will bless the Lord at all times; His praise shall continually be in my mouth." – Psalm 34:1 (ESV)

ACKNOWLEDGEMENTS

I really am done now, I promise. Saying Uncle. Tapping out. Tomorrow, I might be sorry. Wish I'd told more stories. But for today anyway, I mean it. I'm done.

I would, however, like to acknowledge a few folks. Let's start with the One Whom we should all acknowledge first, our Almighty Triune God. Hosea 6:3 says, *"Let us acknowledge the Lord; let us press on to acknowledge Him."* And Solomon reminds his readers in Proverbs 3:6, *"in all your ways acknowledge Him..."* Without the Lord there's no point to any of it, right? All praise to Him.

A massive amount of appreciation goes to my favorite husband Dave, who happens to be the unpaid recipient of all my verbal processing and the forced-labor guinea pig for all my unedited scribbles. And my best friend for sure.

Also, I must acknowledge Marie, without whom I am beyond certain I never would have finished this lengthy self-assignment. You rock, lady. Then there's the other Dave and also Carolyn, who each in turn mentored me well and for years guided me to deep connection with our Heavenly Father.

My acknowledgements would be incomplete if I failed to note the two people who brought me into this world, Ray and Marval Harrison. Raising me how they did and where they did – I am so very, very grateful. Others have encouraged me along the way, by reading my babblings and sharing their thoughts, wisdom and unwavering support: Robynn, Nancy Jo, Ashley, Liz, Don, Mike, Jim, Wally, Clayton. I appreciate you more than you know.

There's no doubt I'm blessed way beyond normal, so much more than average. And I certainly do not deserve all of the other wonderful, incredible people God has placed in my life. You know who you are.

So I close with this: To ALL of you. You who have (perhaps unknowingly) spiced up my mental library with more than enough story content to satisfy my need to share. To each of you I say thank you, thank you. Theoretical hugs all around.

And this poem is for you.

THE GIFT

When I write about you
it is a gift.
It is because
in some way
you strike a chord in me
of warmth and acceptance
of intimacy and poetry
and I feel
good inside.

I thank God for making you
and planting you firmly
in my life.

Because you care
I make it through tough times.
Because you care
I have strength to smile
at life's disappointments.

So when I write about you
it is a gift.
It is because
more than anything
you bring me joy;
And this is the strongest,
deepest,
most real way
I can share with you
how much you mean
to my heart.

Please take this gift,
this appreciation attempt;
Because
YOU
are
a gift
to me.

Hmmm.

To quote the famous fictional teenager, Ferris Bueller, I must ask you this:
"You're still here?"

C'mon, you remember it. At the very end of the movie, after all the credits have scrolled past and everyone in the audience should've already left the theatre, he asks the question I'm asking you.

"You're still here?"

Script (after credits roll):

Ferris > Steps out of the bathroom doorway with a towel on his head. Looks straight at the camera.

"You're still here?" (Shocked face. Moves closer.)

"It's over." (Head shake. Incredulous tone of voice.)

"Go home."

Pause. Retreat from camera. Dismissive hand gesture.

"Go."

www.ingramcontent.com/pod-product-compliance
Lightning Source LLC
Chambersburg PA
CBHW061933271224
19559CB00039B/1278